Some of Freud's Views on
the Sexual Curiosity of Children

"The answers usually given to children in the nursery wound the child's frank and genuine spirit of investigation, and generally deal the first blow at his confidence in his parents; from this time onwards he commonly begins to mistrust grown-up people and keeps to himself what interests him most."

"If it is the purpose of educators to stifle the child's power of independent thought as early as possible, in order to produce that 'good behaviour' which is so highly prized, they cannot do better than deceive children in sexual matters and intimidate them by religious means."

"It is my conviction that no child—none, at least, who is mentally sound, still less one who is mentally gifted—can avoid being occupied with sexual problems in the years *before* puberty."

"The enlightenment which [children] get from one another is frequently mixed with false ideas, and burdened with the remains of older infantile sexual theories. It is scarcely ever complete and sufficient to solve the original problems."

"The stork fable . . . is not one of the infantile sexual theories; indeed, the observation of animals, who hide so little of their sexual life and to whom children feel so closely related, strengthens their disbelief."

Volumes in the Collier Books edition of
The Collected Papers of Sigmund Freud

Each volume has an Introduction by the Editor, Philip Rieff.

The Sexual Enlightenment of Children

SIGMUND FREUD

WITH AN INTRODUCTION BY THE EDITOR

PHILIP RIEFF

COLLIER BOOKS
A Division of Macmillan Publishing Co., Inc.
NEW YORK

Eighth Printing 1978

This Collier Books edition is published by arrangement
with Basic Books, Inc. Macmillan Publishing Co., Inc.,
866 Third Avenue, New York, N.Y. 10022. Collier
Macmillan Canada, Ltd. Printed in the United States
of America.

Contents

Introduction

A HAPPY CHILDHOOD? The idealization of childhood originated in the old literature of the privileged and in the
universal wish of all men, facing the inevitable disappoint-
ments of adulthood, to find something in their past that
was supremely satisfactory. I remember the time when I
happily spun out, for myself, family romances quite like
those Freud discusses in the essay just preceding the case
of "Little Hans" in this volume. Freud has had the major
share in smashing the sentimental cult of the child—sentimental because it is insincere, refusing to take in the depth
of suffering and complexity of thought of which children
are capable. This breaking of the cult of the child has
been to the benefit of children. Sentimentality went with
brutality. For the new sentimentality, in which the child is
given too little sense of the authority of his elders, Freud
is not responsible. On the contrary, the very nucleus of
child training, according to Freud, is the proper accommodation of the child to authority figures. Having made
this accommodation, with Freud's help, "Little Hans" may
be said to have had a reasonably happy childhood.

Hans was a perfectly ordinary little boy; he loved his
mother and had rather more mixed feelings toward his
father. Brighter than most, but otherwise, in Freud's own
term, "normal," Hans exhibited, in his own small and
attractive person, the contradiction that complicates all
human character and renders suspect even our most moral
anxieties. For, according to Freud, the moral sense grows
out of a painful effort to divert our aggressive impulses
from their original objects, by substituting an object that
we imagine is hostile to us. In Hans, this effort at diversion
took the form of a phobia. He feared that horses—any
horse—would bite him; more precisely, that a horse would
bite off his genitals. If that happened, he could no longer
compete with his father for his mother; nor could he be

7

like his father, who was the chief authority of his inner world. Hans's phobia thus had a positive function: it helped him shift his animus from his father to a father-substitute—horses; permitting him to hide his anger and express it, at the same time, and with equally sinister innocence.

Freud did not personally conduct the analysis of this five-year-old boy. Rather, this was, in one sense, the rarest case Freud ever had, one in which the fusion of father and physician became literally true. The analysis was conducted by Hans's father. Thus, in 1909, Freud wrote up a case in which the ideal elements were combined: on the one hand, a pliable, intelligent and dependent patient, on the other, a therapist who showed both the "affectionate care" of a father and the "scientific interest" of an analyst. The case was a complete success.

It was a case that interested Freud specially, not only for its inherent complexity but also because it provided him with his first chance to test inferences about childhood sexuality that were derived, until Hans came along, from the analysis of adults. Since the motives of later neurotic disturbances were rooted in childhood, the case took on a formal importance beyond the immediate exigencies of Hans's personal problems. In fact, the analysis had the effect, according to Freud, of a prophylactic. When Hans came to see him, years later, he was a strapping lad, "normal" in a second and more important sense: he had, with the help of his analyst-father, so outgrown the Oedipal situation that not even the memory of it remained. As the first analysis of a child, the case history of little Hans is precursive of what is now a vast and popular literature. Child analysis carries with it the implicit promise of remission from later miseries that would not otherwise be avoided; it does not carry the promise of remission from those disorders of character which do not appear specifically as symptoms, but rather as an impoverished quality of life. And yet, the case of Hans remains important, for although the way in which Hans exhibited the contradiction in his nature was his own, the contradiction itself is "the common property of all men, a part of the human constitution." To see the contradictions operate so transparently in Hans reveals, in a memorable way, that point of confluence between the particular and the general at which Freud penetrated, more deeply than ever before in our intellectual history, the mystery of the human character.

The ambivalent structure of human nature cannot be altered; but it can be better managed, and the harm we do ourselves can be diminished. Hans learned, during the course of the analysis, really to trust his father, who was the object of his distrust, by the therapeutic process of learning to trust himself, to the point where he no longer feared his own destructive impulses. At that point, his phobia disappeared, for it no longer was needed to protect him from knowing something of the dark side of his own nature.

However, before this success was achieved there was a long game of hide-and-seek, the father seeking the real Hans and Hans avoiding the confrontation with his own instinctual conflict. The game was involved, and highly intellectual. Success was assured when it finally engrossed Hans's attention and his enthusiasm. Thus, this first case study of infantile sexuality was as much a study in infantile intellectuality. Hans's total person had to be engrossed in the effort. The contract in exemplary trust by which the psychoanalytic exploration proceeds needed to be complemented by a contract in exemplary distrust, with the patient trying to take over, for his own defensive purposes, the conduct of the analysis. Hans was a clever little boy, and he fell into the pattern of the game quite willingly. The game consisted in asking all sorts of questions of his parents and other adult authorities, thus opening himself up to counter-questioning. Hans's father and mother, determined disciples of Freud, had a solid respect for the traumatic sequence. They did not discourage him from first believing and then doubting the usual lies: about stork, God and all. Apparently the parents (whom Freud reports as among his "closest adherents") felt duty bound to give Hans the benefit of normal traumas, lest their special know-how untie too quickly the standard knots in the line of libidinal development. This pedant's respect for the inevitability of the traumatic sequence Freud himself shared—if one may surmise from a comment which he made on an incident reported by Hans's father. (Note that the analysis was conducted, with one exception, by correspondence, Freud meeting this youngest among all his patients only once.) When Hans's mother found the child fondling his penis she dutifully threatened: "If you do that, I shall send for Dr. A. to cut off your widdler. And then what'll you widdle with?" Hans's unregenerate reply, so psychoanalytically revealing, was, "With my bottom." Upon this Freud comments heavily: "He made this reply without having any sense of guilt as yet. But this was the occasion of his acquiring the 'castration complex,' the presence of which we are so often obliged to infer in analyzing neurotics, though they one and all struggle violently against recognizing it."

The boy did what he could to help, not yet being old enough to hinder, like an adult neurotic. Near the end of the analysis, he was strongly enough identified with (and residually hostile to) his father-physician to try to take on the chore of communicating, through the mails, with the ultimate father-physician, of whose omniscient presence, just outside the scene, he was aware. "We'll write to the Professor," he announces happily. Dictating some excremental fantasy, he interrupts himself to exclaim, with evident delight at being like his father, "I say, I *am* glad. I'm always so glad when I can write to the Professor." Having grasped the principle that the Professor collects stories relevant to his own sexual interests, Hans took to analysis as a convenient way to further express that interest, within rules acceptable to both sides. When his father gave him a cue with some moralizing reproof ("A good boy doesn't wish that sort of thing."), Hans retorts with theoretic exactitude, "But he may *think* it." To his father's mechanical counterthrust, "But that isn't good," Hans offered, more ingenuously, a new rule, which indicated how fully he was engrossed in the analytic situation: "If he thinks it, it *is* good all the same, because you can write it to the Professor." It was fine sport, this: "Let's write something down for the Professor." The case history shows, here and there, a droll effect, partly because Freud himself seems unaware of the drollery.

Little Hans's cure followed the rationalist Freudian pattern. Remission of his phobic fear of horses followed upon "enlightenment," as Freud calls it. All Hans's anxieties and questions—except the one about the female genitals—were evaded, his fears allowed to ripen (although, of course, Freud understood from the beginning what, in the formulae of the unconscious, "horse" equaled) until the case reached its peripety: the brief single consultation in which son and father sat before Freud and "the Professor," at last in the flesh, revealed to the long-prepared Hans that *Horse* stood in his mind for *Father*. Directly after the visit with Freud, Hans's father noted the first real improvement: the child played in front of the house for an hour, even though horses were passing by. Henceforth, Hans's anxiety abated, although it did not disappear. When, in their trained unwillingness to teach Hans what he must learn at an appropriate time for himself, Hans's parents still hesitated to supply the long-overdue information about the mechanics of birth, Hans took "the analysis into his own hands" by means of "the brilliant symptomatic act" of ripping open a doll. Thereupon his parents knew that this was the propitious time to enlighten him.

As the case ended, after two years in which the game of confronting Hans's contradictory emotions with irenic explanations was played out, the father wrote to Freud that there was just one "unsolved residue." Hans kept "cudgelling his brains to discover what a father has to do with his child, since it is the mother who brings it into the world." On this Freud comments with expected good sense that, had he full and direct charge, he would have explained the father's sexual task to the child, thus completing the resolution.

Hans had characteristics that are always charming in children, less so in adults. In fact, he was already a probationary adult, trying to make choices on the basis of inadequate information. Thus he had a love life—"which showed a very striking degree of inconstancy and a disposition to polygamy." What adult male, in his right mind, has not felt the same disposition, in very striking degree? He was interested in little girls, and he also showed a "trace of homosexuality." In fact, like all children, little Hans was a "positive paragon of all the vices." Yet, of course, Hans was "not by any means a bad character; he was not even one of those children who at his age still give free play to the propensity towards cruelty and violence which is a constituent of human nature." This was an "unusually kind-hearted and affectionate" boy. For this very reason, because he loved his father at the same time that he would have liked to see him dead—he needed a phobic protection against his own impulses. The fear he felt was not generated by horses, or by his father, but by part of himself. Like everyone else in creation, Hans was made up of "pairs of contraries." He could only be relieved of his phobia by excavating to its instinctual source: his death wish toward his father and his sadistic feelings of love toward his mother.

A phobia opposes and restricts both intelligence and sexuality. But this does not mean that in resolving a phobia either intelligence or sexuality are released in some absolute sense. Freud emphasized the contrary. "Analysis does not undo the *effects* of repression." Rather, it "replaces repression by condemnation." Thus the moralizing effect is preserved, while the pathogenic process is replaced by one within the range of personal and conscious control. What is automatic becomes purposeful, what is excessive can be made temperate—but the controls remain; only their side effects are withdrawn. Once having been analyzed, Hans did not then carry out his death wishes against his father or his erotic fantasies of sleeping with his mother. Rather, in Freud's terms, he became both more stable and more civilized, by lowering for himself the cost of acting like a civilized young man.

Unless both the destructive and erotic impulses are brought under the control of consciousness, the moral systems erected upon the unconscious will continue, according to Freud, to work in curious ways, inducing outbursts of immoral action in the name of morality itself. There is, indeed, a streak of nihilism in contemporary radical moralizing precisely because our new moralizers defend the autonomy of the very instincts over which Freud advocated more conscious control. While Freud merely proposed to maintain effective moral control in ways less damaging to our vital energies, some post-Freudians seek to eliminate the moral effect with the repressive cause. In so doing, they are seeking a freedom from both repression and control that is, in the psychoanalytic view, merely another premonitory dream of destruction. If Freud was not a moralizer, in the old sense of supporting repressive symbolic forms, he was also not a nihilist of the new wave, advocating the liberty of the instincts. Sometimes this new instinctualism parades in the uniform of authority, at other times in the literary loincloth of rebellion. In response, Freud tried to create a new authority figure, in the image of the father-physician, helpful, but unwilling to abdicate the moral controls which he both criticizes and yet also represents.

PHILIP RIEFF

University of Pennsylvania
1962

The Sexual Enlightenment of Children

I

The Sexual Enlightenment of Children[1]
(1907)

DEAR SIR—When you ask me for an expression of opinion
on the matter of sexual enlightenment for children, I assume that what you want is the independent opinion of an
individual physician whose professional work offers him
special opportunities for studying the subject, and not a
regular conventional treatise dealing with all the mass of
literature that has grown up around it. I am aware that you
have followed my scientific efforts with interest, and that,
unlike many other colleagues, you do not dismiss my ideas
without a hearing because I regard the psychosexual constitution and certain noxiae in the sexual life as the most
important causes of the neurotic disorders that are so
common. My *Drei Abhandlungen zur Sexualtheorie,* in
which I describe the components of which the sexual instinct is made up, and the disturbances which may occur
in its development into the function of sexuality, has
recently received favourable mention in your Journal.

I am therefore to answer the questions whether children
may be given any information at all in regard to the facts
of sexual life, and at what age and in what way this should
be done. Now let me confess at the outset that discussion
with regard to the second and third points seems to me
perfectly reasonable, but that to my mind it is quite incon-
ceivable how the first of these questions could ever be the
subject of debate. What can be the aim of withholding
from children, or let us say from young people, this information about the sexual life of human beings? Is it a fear

[1] First published in *Soziale Medizin und Hygiene,* Bd. II.,
1907, as an "open letter" to the editor, Dr. M. Fürst; reprinted
in *Sammlung,* Zweite Folge. [Translated by E. B. M. Herford.]

of arousing interest in such matters prematurely, before it spontaneously stirs in them? Is it a hope of retarding by concealment of this kind the development of the sexual instinct in general, until such time as it can find its way into the only channels open to it in the civilized social order? Is it supposed that children would show no interest or understanding for the facts and riddles of sexual life if they were not prompted to do so by outside influence? Is it regarded as possible that the knowledge withheld from them will not reach them in other ways? Or is it genuinely and seriously intended that later on they should consider everything connected with sex as something despicable and abhorrent, from which their parents and teachers wish to keep them apart as long as possible?

I am really at a loss to say which of these can be the motive for the customary concealment from children of everything connected with sex. I only know that these arguments are one and all equally foolish, and that I find it difficult to pay them the compliment of serious refutation. I remember, however, that in the letters of that great thinker and friend of humanity, Multatuli, I once found a few lines which are more than adequate as an answer.[2]

To my mind it seems that certain things are altogether too much wrapped in mystery. It is well to keep the fantasies of children pure, but their purity will not be preserved by ignorance. On the contrary, I believe that concealment leads a girl or boy to suspect the truth more than ever. Curiosity leads to prying into things which would have roused little or no interest if they were talked of openly without any fuss. If this ignorance could be maintained I might be more reconciled to it, but that is impossible; the child comes into contact with other children, books fall into his hands, which lead him to reflect, and the mystery with which things he has already surmised are treated by his parents actually increases his desire to know more. Then this desire that

[2] Multatuli, *Briefe*, 1906, Bd. I. S. 26.

is only incompletely and secretly satisfied gives rise to
excitement and corrupts his imagination, so that the
child is already a sinner while his parents still believe he
does not know what sin is.

I do not know how the case could be better stated,
though perhaps one might amplify it. It is surely nothing
else but habitual prudery and a guilty conscience in themselves about sexual matters which causes adults to adopt
this attitude of mystery towards children; possibly, however, a piece of theoretical ignorance on their part, to be
counteracted only by fresh information, is also responsible.
It is commonly believed that the sexual instinct is lacking
in children, and only begins to arise in them when the
sexual organs mature. This is a grave error, equally serious
from the point of view both of theory and of actual practice. It is so easy to correct it by observation that one can
only wonder how it can ever have arisen. As a matter of
fact, the new-born infant brings sexuality with it into the
world; certain sexual sensations attend its development
while at the breast and during early childhood, and only
very few children would seem to escape some kind of
sexual activity and sexual experiences before puberty. A
more complete exposition of this statement can be found
in my *Drei Abhandlungen zur Sexualtheorie,* to which reference has been made above. The reader will learn that
the specific organs of reproduction are not the only por-
tions of the body which are a source of pleasurable sensation, and that Nature has stringently ordained that even
stimulation of the genitals cannot be avoided during infancy. This period of life, during which a certain degree of
directly sexual pleasure is produced by the stimulation
of various cutaneous areas (erotogenic zones), by the
activity of certain biological impulses and as an accompanying excitation during many affective states, is desig-
nated by an expression introduced by Havelock Ellis as
the period of auto-erotism. Puberty merely brings about
attainment of the stage at which the genitals acquire su-
premacy among all the zones and sources of pleasure, and

in this way presses erotism into the service of reproduction, a process which naturally can undergo certain inhibitions; in the case of those persons who later on become perverts and neurotics this process is only incompletely accomplished. On the other hand, the child is capable long before puberty of most of the mental manifestations of love, for example, tenderness, devotion, and jealousy. Often enough the connection between these mental manifestations and the physical sensation of sexual excitation is so close that the child cannot be in doubt about the relation between the two. To put it briefly, the child is long before puberty a being capable of mature love, lacking only the ability for reproduction; and it may be definitely asserted that the mystery which is set up withholds him only from intellectual comprehension of achievements for which he is psychically and physically prepared.

The intellectual interest of a child in the riddle of sexual life, his desire for knowledge, finds expression at an earlier period of life than is usually suspected. If they have not often come across such cases as I am about to mention, parents must either be afflicted with blindness in regard to this interest in their children, or, when they cannot overlook it, must make every effort to stifle it. I know a splendid boy, now four years old, whose intelligent parents abstain from forcibly suppressing one side of the child's development. Little Herbert, who has certainly not been exposed to any seducing influence from servants, has for some time shown the liveliest interest in that part of his body which he calls his weewee-maker. When only three years old he asked his mother, "Mamma, have you got a weewee-maker, too?" His mother answered, "Of course, what did you think?" He also asked his father the same question repeatedly. At about the same age he was taken to a barn and saw a cow milked for the first time. "Look, milk is coming out of the weewee-maker!" he called in surprise. At the age of three and three-quarters he was well on the way to establish correct categories by means of his own independent observation. He saw how water is run off from a locomotive and said, "See, the engine is making weewee, but where is its weewee-maker?" Later on he added thoughtfully, "Dogs and horses have weewee-makers, but tables and chairs don't have them." Recently he was watching his little sister of one week old being bathed, and remarked, "Her weewee-maker is still tiny; it will get bigger when she grows." (I have heard of this attitude towards the problem of sex difference in other boys of the same age.) I must expressly assert that Herbert is not a sensual child nor even morbidly disposed; in my opinion, since he has never been frightened or oppressed with a sense of guilt, he gives expression quite ingenuously to what he thinks.

The second great problem which exercises a child's mind—probably at a rather later date—is that of the origin of children, and is usually aroused by the un-welcome arrival of a baby brother or sister. This is the oldest and most burning question that assails immature humanity; those who understand how to interpret myths and legends can detect it in the riddle which the Theban Sphinx set to Oedipus. The answers usually given to chil-dren in the nursery wound the child's frank and genuine spirit of investigation, and generally deal the first blow at his confidence in his parents; from this time onwards he commonly begins to mistrust grown-up people and keeps to himself what interests him most. The following letter may show how torturing this very curiosity may become in older children; it was written by a motherless girl of eleven and a half who had been puzzling over the problem with her younger sister.

DEAR AUNT MALI—Please will you be so kind as to write and tell me how you got Chris or Paul. You must know because you are married. We were arguing about it yesterday, and we want to know the truth. We have nobody else to ask. When are you coming to Salzburg? You know, Aunt Mali, we simply can't imagine how the stork brings babies. Trudel thought the stork brings them in a shirt. Then we want to know, too, how the stork gets them out of the pond, and why one never sees babies in ponds. And please will you tell me, too, how you know beforehand when you are going to have one. Please write and tell me *all* about it. Thousands of kisses from all of us.—Your inquiring niece,

LILY.

I do not think that this touching request brought the two sisters the information they wanted. Later on the writer developed the neurosis that arises in unanswered unconscious questions—obsessive speculating.

I do not think that there is even one good reason for denying children the information which their thirst for knowledge demands. To be sure, if it is the purpose of educators to stifle the child's power of independent thought as early as possible, in order to produce that "good behaviour" which is so highly prized, they cannot do better than deceive children in sexual matters and intimidate them by religious means. The stronger characters will, it is true, withstand these influences; they will become rebels against the authority of their parents and later against every other form of authority. When children do not receive the explanations for which they turn to their elders, they go on tormenting themselves in secret with the problem, and produce attempts at solution in which the truth they have guessed is mixed up in the most extraordinary way with grotesque inventions; or else they whisper confidences to each other which, because of the sense of guilt in the youthful inquirers, stamp everything sexual as horrible and disgusting. These infantile sexual theories are well worth collecting and examining. After these experiences children usually lose the only proper attitude to sexual questions, many of them never to find it again.

It would seem that the overwhelming majority of writers, both men and women, who have dealt with the question of explaining sexual matters to children have expressed themselves in favour of enlightenment. The clumsiness, however, of most of their proposals how and when this enlightenment should be carried out leads one to conclude that they have not found it very easy to venture this admission. As far as my knowledge of the literature goes, the charming letter of explanation which a certain Frau Emma Eckstein gives as written to her ten-year-old boy stands out conspicuously.[3] The customary method is obviously not the right one. All sexual knowledge is kept from children as long as possible, and then on one single occasion an explanation, which is even then only half the truth and generally comes too late, is proffered them in mysterious and solemn language. Most of the answers to the question "How can I tell my children?" make such a pitiful impression, at least upon me, that I should prefer parents not to concern themselves with the explanation at all. It is much more important that children should never get the idea that one wants to make more of a secret of the facts of sexual life than of any other matter not suited to their understanding. To ensure this it is necessary that from the very beginning everything sexual should be treated like everything else that is worth knowing about. Above all, schools should not evade the task of mentioning sexual matters; lessons about the animal kingdom should include the great facts of reproduction, which should be given their due significance, and emphasis should be laid at the same time on the fact that man shares with the higher animals everything essential to his organization. Then, if the atmosphere of the home does not make for suppression of all reasoning, something similar to what I once overheard in a nursery would probably occur oftener. A small boy said to his little sister, "How can you think the stork brings babies! You know that man is a mammal, do you suppose that storks bring other mammals their young too?" In this way the curiosity of children will never become very intense, for at each stage in its inquiries it will find the satisfaction it needs. Explanations about the specific circumstances of human sexuality and some indica-

[3] Emma Eckstein, *Die Sexualfrage in der Erziehung des Kindes,* 1904.

tion of its social significance should be provided before the child is eleven years old.[4] The age of confirmation would be a more suitable time than any other at which to instruct the child, who already has full knowledge of the physical facts involved, in those social obligations which are bound up with the actual gratification of this instinct. A gradual and progressive course of instruction in sexual matters such as this, at no period interrupted, in which the school takes the initiative, seems to me to be the only method of giving the necessary information that takes into consideration the development of the child and thus successfully avoids ever-present dangers.

I consider it a most significant advance in the science of education that in France, in place of the catechism, the State should have introduced a primer which gives the child his first instruction in his position as a citizen and in the ethical obligations which will be his in time to come. The elementary instruction provided there, however, is seriously deficient in that it includes no reference to sexual matters. Here is the omission which stands in such need of attention on the part of educators and reformers. In those countries which leave the education of children either wholly or in part in the hands of the priesthood, the method urged would of course not be practicable. No priest will ever admit the identity in nature of man and beast, since to him the immortality of the soul is a foundation for moral training which he cannot forgo. Here again we clearly see the unwisdom of putting new wine into old bottles, and perceive the impossibility of carrying through a reform in one particular without altering the foundations of the whole system.

[4] [The original has also: *am Schlusse des Volksschulunterrichtes und vor Eintritt in die Mittelschule.*—Trans.]

II

On the Sexual Theories of Children[1]
(1908)

THE MATERIAL on which the following synthesis is built up is derived from many sources. First, from the direct observation of what children say and do; secondly, from what adult neurotics consciously remember of their childhood and retail during psychoanalytic treatment; and thirdly, from the conclusions, reconstructions and unconscious memories translated into consciousness which result from the psychoanalysis of neurotics.

That the first of these three sources has not alone supplied all that is worth knowing on the subject is due to the attitude of adults towards childish sexual life. Children are not credited with any sexual activities, therefore no pains are taken to observe anything of the kind, while on the other hand any expressions of such a thing which would be worthy of attention are suppressed. Consequently the opportunity of gaining information from this most genuine and fertile source is greatly restricted. Whatever we derive from the uninfluenced communications of adults concerning their conscious childhood is at best subject to the objection that it is perhaps falsified in looking back and, further, has to be estimated in the light of the fact that the persons in question have later become neurotic. The material from the third source is subject to all the attacks that are in general directed against the trustworthiness of psychoanalysis and the reliability of the conclusions drawn from it, so that no justification of it can be attempted here; I will only assert that those who know and

---

[1] First published in *Sexualprobleme*, new issue of the periodical *Mutterschutz*, Bd. IV., 1908; reprinted in *Sammlung, Zweite Folge.* [Translated by Douglas Bryan.]

make use of the psychoanalytic technique acquire extensive confidence in its results.

I cannot guarantee the completeness of my collection, but I can answer for the care taken in gathering the material.

There remains a difficult question to decide. How far ought one to take for granted what is here reported about children in general as being true of all children, *i.e.* of every individual child? Pressure of education and the varying intensity of the sexual instinct certainly render possible great individual variations in the sexual behaviour of children, and, above all, these things influence the date at which the childish interest in sexuality appears. Therefore I have not arranged my material according to the successive epochs of childhood, but have included in one recital what applies to various children, in one early, and in another late. It is my conviction that no child—none, at least, who is mentally sound, still less one who is mentally gifted—can avoid being occupied with sexual problems in the years *before* puberty.

I do not think much of the objection that neurotics are a special class of people marked by a degenerative disposition, whose child-life must not be regarded as evidence of the childhood of others. Neurotics are human beings like every one else, and cannot be sharply differentiated from normal people; in their childhood they are not easily distinguishable from those who later remain healthy. It is one of the most valuable results of our psychoanalytic investigations to have found that their neuroses have no special mental content peculiar to them, but that, as C. G. Jung has expressed it, they fall ill of the same complexes with which we who are healthy also have to contend. The difference is only that the healthy know how to overcome these complexes without great and practically demonstrable harm; while the suppression of these complexes in nervous people only succeeds at the price of costly substitute-formations, thus in practice proving unsuccessful. In childhood nervous and normal people naturally approximate much more closely than in later life, so that I cannot recognize it as an error in method to make use of the communications of neurotics concerning their childhood as analogies for normal child-life. Since those who later become neurotics very frequently include in their constitution an especially strong sexual instinct and a disposition to precocity and to premature expression of this impulse, they enable us in this way to recognize much of the infantile sexual activities more plainly and more correctly than, with our blunted talent for observation of ordinary children, would otherwise be possible. The true value of these communications by adult neurotics can only be estimated, to be sure, when a collection of the childhood-memories of adult healthy people, made after the manner of Havelock Ellis, has also been taken into account.

In consequence of both external and internal unfavourable circumstances, the following remarks apply chiefly to the sexual development of one sex only, namely, the male. The value of a compilation such as I attempt here, however, need not be merely descriptive. The knowledge of the infantile sexual theories in the form in which they appear in childish thoughts can be of interest in various directions—for instance, surprisingly so for an understanding of myths and fairy-tales. They are indispensable for the understanding of the neuroses, where these childish theories are still in operation and have acquired a determining influence upon the form taken by the symptoms.

If, forgetting our mortality and imagining ourselves to be merely thinking beings, gazing, for instance, from another planet, we could apprehend the things of this earth afresh, perhaps nothing would arrest our attention more forcibly than the existence of two sexes among human beings, who otherwise resemble each other so closely and yet emphasize their difference even in the most superficial indications. Now it does not seem that children also choose this fundamental fact as the starting-point of their investigations concerning sexual problems. Since they have known a father and a mother as far back as they can remember in life, they accept their existence as a reality which needs no further inquiry, and in just the same way does a boy behave towards a little sister from whom he is only separated by a slight difference of age, by one or two years. The child's desire for knowledge does not awaken spontaneously on this point at all, as it would if prompted perhaps by an inborn need to seek for causes, but arises under the goad of a self-seeking impulse which dominates him when he is confronted by the arrival of a new child— perchance at the end of the second year. Those children whose own nursery at home does not become divided up in this way are nevertheless able as a result of their own observations to put themselves in the place of others who are in this situation in other homes. The loss of the parents' care and concern, which they actually experience or with justice fear, the presentiment that they must from now and for ever share all possessions with the newcomer, have the effect of awakening the emotions of the child and sharpening its thinking capacities. The elder child expresses unconcealed hostility against the newcomer, which finds vent in unfriendly criticisms of it, in wishes that "the stork should take it back again," and occasionally even in attempts at little outrages upon the helpless creature lying in the cradle. A greater difference of age as a rule modifies the expression of this primary hostility; just as in somewhat later years, if brothers and sisters fail to appear, the wish for a playmate like those observed elsewhere obtains the upper hand.

Under the stimulus of these feelings and anxieties the child thus comes to consider the first of the great problems of life, and asks itself the question where children come from, which at first runs, "Where did this particular tiresome child come from?" The after-echo of this first riddle seems to be observable in the innumerable riddles of myths and sagas. The question itself, like all inquiry, is a product of dire necessity, as if to thought were entrusted the task of preventing the repetition of an event so greatly feared. At the same time, we may assume, the child's thinking becomes independent of the stimulus, and continues its activity as a separate impulse towards investigation. Where a child is not already too much intimidated, it takes sooner or later the shortest way by demanding answers from its parents or attendants, who signify for it the source of all knowledge. This way, however, fails. The child receives either evasive answers or a rebuke for its curiosity, or is dismissed with that mythologically significant information which in German runs: "The stork brings the children; it fetches them out of the water." I have grounds for supposing that far more children than parents suspect are dissatisfied with this solution, and respond to it with pronounced doubt, which, however, is not always outspoken. I know of a three-year-old boy who, to the terror of his nurse, was missed after receiving this enlightenment, and found at the edge of the big lake of the castle, where he had run, in order to see the children in the water! I know of another who could allow his disbelief only hesitating expression by saying he knew better, it was not storks who bring the children, but herons. It appears to me from much of the evidence conclusive that children refuse to believe the stork theory, and that from the time of this first deception and rebuff they nourish a mistrust against adults, have the presentiment of something forbidden which is being withheld from them by the "grown-ups," and consequently conceal their further investigations by secrecy. With this, however, it comes about that they experience the first occasion of a "psychical conflict," in that ideas for which they "by instinct" feel a preference, but which adults consider "naughty," come into opposition with others which are maintained by the authority of the adults without being acceptable to them themselves. Out of these mental conflicts there may soon arise a "mental dissociation"; the one idea which is bound up with "being good," but also with a cessation of thinking, becomes the prevailing conscious one; the other, for which meanwhile the inquiries prosecuted have brought new evidence, which is not supposed to count, becomes suppressed and unconscious. The nuclear complex of neurosis is formed in this way.

Lately, by the analysis of a five-year-old boy[2] which his father undertook and permitted me to publish, I have received an irrefutable proof of a piece of knowledge towards which the psychoanalysis of adults had for long led me. I now know that the changes in the mother during pregnancy do not escape the sharp eyes of a child, and that the latter is very well able subsequently to establish the correct connection between the increase in size of the mother's body and the appearance of a baby. In the case mentioned, the boy was three and a half when his sister was born, and four and three-quarters when he showed his better knowledge by the most unmistakable allusions. This precocious knowledge is, however, always kept secret, and later, in connection with the future fate of childish sexual inquiry, is repressed and forgotten.

The stork fable, therefore, is not one of the infantile sexual theories; indeed, the observation of animals, who hide so little of their sexual life and to whom children feel so closely related, strengthens their disbelief. With the knowledge independently obtained that babies grow in the mother's body, a child would be on the right path to solve the problem on which it first tries its thinking powers. Its further progress is stopped, however, by a piece of ignorance which cannot be made good, and by false theories which the condition of its own sexuality imposes on it.

These false sexual theories, which I will now describe, all have one very curious characteristic. Although they go astray in a grotesque way, yet they all, each one of them, contain a bit of the real truth, so that they are analogous to those adult attempts at solution, which we call flashes of genius, of the problems of the universe that are too difficult for human comprehension. What is correct and hits the mark in these theories is to be explained by their origin in those components of the sexual instinct which are already active in the childish organism; for it is not due to an arbitrary mental act or to chance impressions that

[2] *Infra*, Freud, "Analysis of a Phobia in a Five-year-old Boy."

these notions arise, but to the necessities of the psycho-sexual constitution, and this is why we are able to speak of typical sexual theories in children, this is why we find the same false ideas in all children whose sexual life is accessible to us.

The first of these theories begins with a neglect of sex-differentiation, the neglect to which we called special attention at the commencement as being characteristic of children. It consists in attributing to everybody, including women, a penis just like the one the boy knows of from his own body. It is precisely in that sexual constitution which we must recognize as a normal one that the penis is already in childhood the governing erotogenic zone, the most important auto-erotic sexual object, and the estimate of its value is logically reflected in the impossibility of imagining a person similar to the self without this essential part. If a little boy obtains a sight of the genitals of a little sister, what he says will show that his prejudice is already strong enough to influence the perception; he does not remark on the lack of the penis but *invariably* says, as if consoling and reconciling: that her "widdler" is still small, but when she is bigger it will soon grow. The idea of a woman with a penis returns still later in the dreams of adults; in a state of nocturnal sexual excitation he throws down a woman, exposes her and prepares for coitus; then on beholding the well-formed penis at the site of the female genitals, the dream and excitation break off. The numerous hermaph-rodites of classic antiquity faithfully reproduce this once general infantile idea; one may observe that to most normal people they cause no offence, while actual hermaph-roditic formations of the genitals in nature nearly always excite the greatest abhorrence.

If this idea of woman with a penis becomes "fixated" in a child, it resists all the influences of later life and makes the man incapable of dispensing with a penis in his sexual object, so that such a person, if otherwise he has a normal sexual life, must become homosexual, seeking his sexual object in men who through other physical and mental qualities remind him of women. Real women, as they become known to him later, are excluded from being sexual objects to him because they lack the essential sexual attraction; indeed, in connection with another impression of childhood-life they may become abhorrent to him. A child who is chiefly dominated by penis-excitation usually produces pleasure by stimulation of it with his hand, is detected doing this by his parents or by the persons in charge of him, and is terrorized by the threat that his penis will be cut off. The effect of this "castration threat" is in direct proportion to the value set upon this part of the body, *i.e.,* quite extraordinarily deep-rooted and persistent. Sagas and myths testify to the revolt in the childish feelings, to the horror which is then linked to the castration complex, and this later is remembered with corresponding reluctance by consciousness. The woman's genitalia, seen subsequently and regarded as mutilated, recall this threat, and thus awaken in the homosexual horror instead of pleasure. This reaction is not altered by his learning through science that the childish assumption is not so far wrong after all, namely, that a woman also possesses a penis. Anatomy has recognized the clitoris within the female pudenda as an organ homologous to the penis, and the physiology of sexual processes has been able to add that this little penis which no longer grows behaves in the childhood of the woman like a genuine and real penis, that it is the site of excitations which leads to its being touched, that its excitability gives the sexual activity of little girls a male character, and that it needs an effort of repression in the years of puberty to make the woman develop through discarding this male sexuality. The fact that the sexual function of many women is crippled by their obstinately clinging to this clitoris excitability—so that they remain anæsthetic in coitus, or that repression succeeds so excessively that its action is partly nullified by hysterical compensatory formations—all this shows that the infantile sexual theory that a woman possesses a penis like a man has some truth in it.

One can easily observe that little girls are quite in agreement with their brothers' estimate. They develop a great interest in this part of a boy's body, but this interest is at once dominated by jealousy. They feel themselves injured; they make attempts to urinate in the position that is possible to the boy by his possession of the big penis, and when they express the wish, "I should love to be a boy," we know what lack the wish is to remedy.

If children could follow the hint given them by the excitation in the penis, they would get a little nearer to the solution of their problems. That the baby grows in the mother's body is obviously not a sufficient explanation. How does it get there? What starts it developing there? That the father has something to do with it is probable; indeed, he declares that the baby is also *his* child.[8] The penis, too, certainly also has its share in these mysterious happenings; it testifies to this by the accompanying excitation in it during all this thought-work. Along with this excitation obscure impulses are roused, which the child does not know how to account for—to do something violent, to press in, to knock to pieces, to burst open a hole somewhere. But when the child seems thus in a fair way to arrive at the existence of the vagina, and to attribute to the father's penis an act of incursion into the mother which should create the baby in the body of the mother, the inquiry breaks off helplessly; for at this point there stands in the way the theory that the mother possesses a penis like a man, and the existence of the cavity which receives the penis remains undiscovered to the child. One can readily surmise that the lack of success of this effort of thought facilitates a rejection and forgetting of it. These speculations and doubts, however, become the prototype of all later thought-work on problems, and the first failure has a crippling effect for ever after.

Their ignorance of the vagina again makes it possible for children to have a conviction which constitutes the second of their sexual theories. If the baby grows in the body of the mother and is then detached from it, this can only happen by the sole possible way of the anal aperture.

[8] Freud, *op. cit.*

The child must be expelled like excrement, like a move-ment. If in later childhood the same question is the subject of solitary reflection or of a discussion between two children, then the explanations probably are that the baby comes out of the navel, which opens, or that the belly is slit and the child taken out, as happens to the wolf in the tale of Little Red Riding-Hood. These theories are expressed aloud and later consciously remembered; they no longer contain anything shocking. These same children have then completely forgotten that in earlier years they believed another sexual theory, which since then has undergone the subsequent repression of the anal sexual components. At that time an evacuation was something which could be spoken about in the nursery without shame; the child was still not so far distant from his constitutional coprophilic inclinations; it was no degradation then to come into the world like a mass of fæces, which had not yet been attainted by disgust. The *cloaca* theory, which is valid for so many animals, was the most natural and the only one which could force itself upon the child as probable.

Then, however, it was only logical that the child should refuse to grant women the painful monopoly of giving birth to children. If babies are born through the anus then a man can give birth just as well as a woman. A boy can therefore fancy that he too has children of his own without our needing to accuse him of feminine inclinations. It is only his still active anal erotism at work.

If the cloaca theory of birth is preserved in consciousness in later years of childhood, which occasionally happens, it is then accompanied by another solution of the question concerning the origin of children, one which, it is true, is no longer the original one. It is like that in fairy-tales. One eats some particular thing and from this one gets a child. The insane re-animate this infantile birth theory. A maniac, for instance, will lead the visiting physician to a heap of fæces which she has deposited in a corner of her cell, and say to him, laughing, "That is the child I bore to-day."

The third of the typical sexual theories appears in

children when through some unforeseen domestic occurrence they witness parental sexual intercourse, concerning which they are then able to obtain only a very incomplete idea. Whatever detail it may be that comes under their observation, whether it is the position of the two people, or the sounds, or certain accessory circumstances, in all cases they arrive at the same conclusion, that is, at what we may call the *sadistic conception of coitus,* seeing in it something that the stronger person inflicts on the weaker by force, and comparing it, especially the boy, to a fight as they know it from their childish play, in which, by the way, an admixture of sexual excitation is also not wanting. I have not been able to establish whether children recognize this procedure which they observe between the parents as the necessary missing link in the problem of the birth of children; more often it appears that this connection is overlooked by children for the very reason that they had interpreted the love-act as an act of violence. But this sadistic conception itself gives the impression of a reappearance of that obscure impulse towards cruel activity which was linked up with penis-excitation when the child first reflected upon the puzzle of where children come from. The possibility cannot be excluded that that precocious sadistic impulse, which might have led to discovery of the mystery of coitus, itself appeared first under the influence of very dim memories of parental intercourse for which the child had obtained material, without at the time making use of it, when it shared the bedroom of its parents in the first years of its life.[4]

The sadistic theory of coitus, which by itself becomes a false guide where it might have led to enlightenment, is again the expression of one of the inborn components of the sexual instinct, any one of which may be more or less strongly marked in any particular child, and thus the

[4] In his autobiographical book entitled *Monsieur Nicolas,* published in 1794, this sadistic misconception of coitus is confirmed by Restif de la Bretonne, who there relates an experience from his fourth year.

sadistic conception is to a certain extent true; in part it divines the essence of the sexual act and the "antagonism of the sexes" which precedes it. Often, too, the child is in a position to support this conception by accidental observations which it understands in part correctly, in part falsely. In many marriages the wife, in fact, regularly opposes the matrimonial embrace, which to her brings no pleasure and the risk of a fresh pregnancy, and thus to the child who is supposed to be asleep (or pretending to be asleep) the mother might give an impression that could only be explained as meaning warding off an act of violence. At other times the whole marriage presents to the observant child the spectacle of an unceasing quarrel, expressed by loud words and unfriendly gestures, so that the child need not wonder that this quarrel goes on in the night, too, and is finally decided by the very same means which the child himself is accustomed to make use of in its intercourse with its brothers, sisters and companions, that is, by a fight.

The child also regards it as a confirmation of his idea if he discovers spots of blood in the bed or on his mother's linen. These are to him a proof that in the night an attack of this kind by the father on the mother has again taken place, while we should rather take the fresh spots of blood to mean that sexual intercourse for the time being had ceased. Much of the inexplicable "horror of blood" in the nervous finds its explanation in this connection. The child's mistake again covers a small part of the truth, for in certain well-known circumstances a trace of blood is indeed regarded as a sign of initiated sexual intercourse.

In less direct connection with the insoluble problem of where children come from, the child occupies itself with the question of what the nature and the content is of the state called "being married"; and it answers the question differently according to its accidental observations of its parents combined with its own impulses which are still invested with pleasurable feeling. All that these answers appear to have in common is that marriage promises pleasurable gratification, and presupposes a disregard for modesty. The idea I have most frequently met with is that "one urinates before the other"; a variation of this which sounds as if it signified better knowledge symbolically is that "the man urinates into the woman's chamber." On other occasions the meaning of marriage is supposed to be that the two persons show their buttocks to each other (without shame). In one case in which training had succeeded in postponing sexual knowledge especially late, a fourteen-year-old girl who had already begun to menstruate arrived at the idea from reading that being married signified "mixing blood," and since her own sister had not yet had a period the lustful girl attempted to outrage a visitor who confessed that she was just menstruating, so as to compel her to take part in this "mixing blood."

The infantile ideas about the nature of marriage, which are not seldom retained by the conscious memory, have great significance for the symptoms of later neurotic illness. They come into evidence first of all in childish games, in which one does with the other whatever it is that constitutes being married, and then later on the wish to be married can choose the infantile form of expression when it appears in a phobia or some similar symptom which at first sight seemed incomprehensible.[5]

These are the most important of the typical sexual theories that children produce spontaneously in early childhood-years under the influence of the components of the sexual instinct. I know that the material is far from complete and that I have not established a full connection between it and the rest of child-life. I can here add a few supplementary remarks which otherwise every experienced person would have missed in my account. Thus, for instance, the significant theory that one gets a child by a kiss, which obviously betrays a pre-eminence of the erotogenic mouth zone. In my experience this theory is exclusively feminine and is sometimes met with as pathogenic in girls whose sexual curiosity had undergone very

[5] The games that are significant in later neuroses are the "doctor" game and the game of "father and mother."

strong inhibition in childhood. One of my female patients through an accidental observation happened upon the theory of the "couvade," which is well known among many races as a general practice, and probably has the purpose of contradicting that doubt about paternity that is never quite to be overcome. After the birth of his child, a rather strange uncle of hers remained for days at home and received visitors in his night-shirt, so she concluded that both parents had a share in the birth and must go to bed.

About the tenth or eleventh year information about sexual matters comes to children. A child who has grown up unchecked in its social relations, or who in some other way has found a good opportunity for observation, communicates to other children what he knows, because by doing so he can feel himself to be grown-up and superior. What children learn in this way is mostly correct, that is, the existence of the vagina and its use is revealed to them, but otherwise the enlightenment which they get from one another is frequently mixed with false ideas, and burdened with the remains of older infantile sexual theories. It is scarcely ever complete and sufficient to solve the original problems. Just as formerly with the ignorance of the vagina, so now ignorance of the semen prevents understanding of the whole process. The child cannot guess that out of the male sexual organ another substance can be expelled besides urine, and occasionally an "innocent" girl on her wedding night is still indignant because the man has "urinated into her." This information acquired before puberty links up with a fresh impetus in childish inquiries; the theories which the child now produces, however, have no longer the typical and original stamp, which was characteristic of the early primary ones as long as the infantile sexual components were uninhibited and untransformed and could come to expression in these theories. The later intellectual efforts to solve the sexual puzzle seemed to me not worth the trouble of collecting, nor have they much claim to a pathogenic significance. Their multiplicity is naturally mainly dependent upon the nature of the first information received, their significance consists rather in that they re-awaken the unconscious vestiges of that first period of sexual interest, so that not seldom masturbatory sexual activities and a part of the detachment of feeling from the parents is linked up with them. Hence the condemning judgement of teachers that such information at this age "corrupts" children.

A few examples may show what elements often enter into these later speculations by children about sexual life. A girl had heard from her school companions that the man gives the woman an egg, which she hatches in her body. A boy who had also heard of the egg, identified it with the testicle, which is vulgarly called by the same name, and thereupon puzzled his head how the content of the scrotum could always become renewed. The information given seldom reaches as far as to prevent important doubts on the matter of sexual processes. Thus girls may come to expect that coitus happens only on one single occasion but lasts very long, for twenty-four hours, and that from this one occasion come all the successive children. One would suppose that this child had knowledge of the process of propagation in certain insects: however, this conjecture was not confirmed and the theory appeared to be an independent creation. Other girls ignore the time of gestation, the life in the womb, and suppose that the child appears immediately after the night of the first connection. Marcel Prévost has turned this mistake of young girls into an amusing story in one of his *Lettres de femmes*. Hardly to be exhausted and perhaps in general not uninteresting is this theme of the later sexual inquiries of children, or of adolescents who have been delayed at a childish stage; but it lies further from my purpose, and I must only call special attention to the fact that many errors are invented by children in order to contradict older, better but now unconscious and repressed knowledge.

The way in which the child behaves when he receives information also has its significance. In many children sexual repression has gone so far that they will not hear anything, and these may also succeed in remaining ignorant until even later (apparently, at least) till the knowledge dating from early childhood comes to light in the psychoanalysis of neurotics. I know also of two boys between ten and thirteen years old, who certainly listened to sexual information but gave their informant the averting answer: "It is possible that your father and other people do such things, but I know for certain that my father would never do it." However this later attitude in children towards satisfying their sexual curiosity may vary, we can postulate a thoroughly uniform behaviour in them in early years and believe that at that period they were all eager to find out what it is the parents do with each other to make the babies.

III

Family Romances[1] (1908)[2]

THE FREEING of an individual, as he grows up, from the
authority of his parents is one of the most necessary
though one of the most painful results brought about by
the course of his development. It is quite essential that that
liberation should occur and it may be presumed that it has
been to some extent achieved by everyone who has reached
a normal state. Indeed, the whole progress of society rests
upon the opposition between successive generations. On
the other hand, there is a class of neurotics whose condition is recognizably determined by their having failed in
this task.

For a small child his parents are at first the only
authority and the source of all belief. The child's most
intense and most momentous wish during these early years
is to be like his parents (that is, the parent of his own sex)
and to be big like his father and mother. But as intellectual
growth increases, the child cannot help discovering by
degrees the category to which his parents belong. He gets
to know other parents and compares them with his own,
and so comes to doubt the incomparable and unique
quality which he has attributed to them. Small events in
the child's life which make him feel dissatisfied afford him
provocation for beginning to criticize his parents, and for

[1] [Otto Rank's book *Der Mythus von der Geburt des Helden*
(1909) included this note by Freud, which was reprinted
under the title of "Der Familienroman der Neurotiker," *Ges.
Schr.*, 12, 367, and *Ges. W.*, 7, 227. Rank's book appeared in
English as *The Myth of the Birth of the Hero* (1914). Present
translation by James Strachey.]

[2] Probable date of composition.—P. R.

using, in order to support his critical attitude, the knowledge which he has acquired that other parents are in some respects preferable to them. The psychology of the neuroses teaches us that, among other factors, the most intense impulses of sexual rivalry contribute to this result. A feeling of being slighted is obviously what constitutes the subject-matter of such provocations. There are only too many occasions on which a child is slighted, or at least *feels* he has been slighted, on which he feels he is not receiving the whole of his parents' love, and, most of all, on which he feels regrets at having to share it with brothers and sisters. His sense that his own affection is not being fully reciprocated then finds a vent in the idea, which is often consciously recollected from early childhood, of being a step-child or an adopted child. People who have not developed neuroses very frequently remember occasions of this kind on which—usually as a result of something they have read—they thus interpreted and responded to their parents' hostile behaviour. But at this point the influence of sex is already in evidence, for a boy is far more inclined to feel hostile impulses towards his father than towards his mother and has a far more intense desire to get free from *him* than from *her*. In this respect the imagination of girls is apt to show itself much weaker. These consciously remembered mental impulses of childhood embody the factor which enables us to understand the nature of hero-myths.

The later stage in the development of the neurotic's estrangement from his parents, begun in this manner, might be described as "the neurotic's family romance." It is seldom remembered consciously but can almost always be revealed by psychoanalysis. For a quite specific form of imaginative activity is one of the essential characteristics of neurotics and also of all comparatively highly gifted people. This activity emerges first in children's play, and then, starting roughly from the period before puberty, takes over the topic of family relations. A characteristic example of this particular kind of phantasy is to be seen in the familiar day-dreams[3] which persist far beyond puberty. If these day-dreams are carefully examined, they are found to serve as the fulfilment of wishes and as a correction of actual life. They have two principal aims, erotic and ambitious—though an erotic aim is usually concealed behind the latter too. At about the period I have mentioned, then, the child's imagination becomes engaged in the task of getting free from the parents of whom he now has such a low opinion and of replacing them by others, occupying, as a rule, a higher social station. He will make use in this connection of any opportune coincidences from his actual experience, such as his becoming acquainted with the Lord of the Manor or some landed proprietor if he lives in the country or with some member of the aristocracy if he lives in town. Chance occurrences of this kind arouse the child's envy, which finds expression in a phantasy in which both his parents are replaced by others of better birth. The technique used in carrying out phantasies like this (which are, of course, conscious at this period) depends upon the ingenuity and the material which the child has at his disposal. There is also the question of whether the phantasies are worked out with greater or less effort to obtain verisimilitude. This stage is reached at a time at which the child is still in ignorance of the sexual determinants of procreation.

When presently the child comes to know of the various kinds of sexual relations between fathers and mothers and realizes that "*pater semper incertus est*," while the mother is "*certissima*," the family romance undergoes a peculiar curtailment: it contents itself with exalting the child's father, but no longer casts any doubts on his maternal origin, which is regarded as something unalterable. This second (sexual) stage of the family romance is actuated

[3] Cf. "Hysterical Phantasies and their Relation to Bisexuality," *Dora—Analysis of a Case of Hysteria,* Collier Books edition AS 581V, where a reference will be found to the literature of the subject.

by another motive as well, which is absent in the first (asexual) stage. The child, having learnt about sexual processes, tends to picture to himself erotic situations and relations, the motive force behind this being his desire to bring his mother (who is the subject of the most intense sexual curiosity) into situations of secret infidelity and into secret love-affairs. In this way the child's phantasies, which started by being, as it were, asexual, are brought up to the level of his later knowledge.

Moreover the motive of revenge and retaliation, which was in the background at the earlier stage, is also to be found at the later one. It is, as a rule, precisely these neurotic children who were punished by their parents for sexual naughtiness and who later revenge themselves on their parents by means of phantasies of this kind.

A younger child is very specially inclined to use imaginative stories such as these in order to rob those born before him of their prerogatives—in a way which reminds one of historical intrigues; and he often has no hesitation in attributing to his mother as many fictitious love-affairs as he himself has competitors. An interesting variant of the family romance may then appear, in which the hero and author returns to legitimacy himself while his brothers and sisters are got out of the way by being bastardized. So too if there are any other particular interests at work they can direct the course to be taken by the family romance; for its many-sidedness and its great range of applicability enable it to meet every sort of requirement. In this way, for instance, the young phantasy-builder can get rid of his forbidden degree of kinship with one of his sisters if he finds himself sexually attracted by her.

If anyone is inclined to turn away in horror from this depravity of the childish heart or feels tempted, indeed, to dispute the possibility of such things, he should observe that these works of fiction, which seem so full of hostility, are none of them really so badly intended, and that they still preserve, under a slight disguise, the child's original affection for his parents. The faithlessness and ingratitude are only apparent. If we examine in detail the commonest of these imaginative romances, the replacement of both parents or of the father alone by grander people, we find that these new and aristocratic parents are equipped with attributes that are derived entirely from real recollections of the actual and humble ones; so that in fact the child is not getting rid of his father but exalting him. Indeed the whole effort at replacing the real father by a superior one is only an expression of the child's longing for the happy, vanished days when his father seemed to him the noblest and strongest of men and his mother the dearest and loveliest of women. He is turning away from the father whom he knows to-day to the father in whom he believed in the earlier years of his childhood; and his phantasy is no more than the expression of a regret that those happy days have gone. Thus in these phantasies the over-valuation that characterizes a child's earliest years comes into its own again. An interesting contribution to this subject is afforded by the study of dreams. We learn from their interpretation that even in later years, if the Emperor and Empress appear in dreams, those exalted personages stand for the dreamer's father and mother.[4] So that the child's over-valuation of his parents also survives in the dreams of normal adults.

[4] Cf. my *Interpretation of Dreams* (1900). [English translation, revised ed. (1932), 336.]

IV

Analysis of a Phobia in a
Five-Year-Old Boy[1] (1909)

1. Introduction

IN THE FOLLOWING PAGES I propose to describe the course
of the illness and recovery of a very youthful patient.
The case history is not, strictly speaking, derived from
my observation. It is true that I laid down the general
lines of the treatment, and that on one single occasion,
when I had a conversation with the boy, I took a direct
share in it; but the treatment itself was carried out by the
child's father, and it is to him that I owe my sincerest
thanks for allowing me to publish his notes upon the case.
But his services go further than this. No one else, in my
opinion, could possibly have prevailed on the child to
make any such avowals; the special knowledge by means
of which he was able to interpret the remarks made by his
five-year-old son was indispensable, and without it the
technical difficulties in the way of conducting a psychoanalysis upon so young a child would have been insuper-
able. It was only because the authority of a father and of a
physician were united in a single person, and because in
him both affectionate care and scientific interest were combined, that it was possible in this one instance to apply
the method to a use to which it would not otherwise have
lent itself.

But the peculiar value of this observation lies in the
considerations which follow. When a physician treats an
adult neurotic by psychoanalysis, the process he goes

[1] [First published in *Jahrbuch für psychoanalytische und
psychopathologische Forschungen*, Bd. i., 1909. Reprinted in
Freud, *Sammlung kleiner Schriften*, ii., 1913.]

through of uncovering the psychical formations, layer by layer, eventually enables him to frame certain hypotheses as to the patient's infantile sexuality; and it is in the components of the latter that he believes he has discovered the motive forces of all the neurotic symptoms of later life. I have set out these hypotheses in my *Drei Abhandlungen zur Sexualtheorie* (published in 1905), and I am aware that they seem as strange to an outside reader as they seem inevitable to a psychoanalyst. But even a psychoanalyst may confess to the wish for a more direct and less roundabout proof of these fundamental theorems. Surely there must be a possibility of observing upon the child at first hand and in all the freshness of life the sexual impulses and conative tendencies which we dig out so laboriously in the adult from among their own débris—especially as it is also our belief that they are the common property of all men, a part of the human constitution, and merely exaggerated or distorted in the case of neurotics.

With this end in view I have for many years been urging my pupils and my friends to collect observations on the sexual life of children—the existence of which has as a rule been cleverly overlooked or deliberately denied. Among the material which came into my possession as a result of these requests, the reports which I received at regular intervals about little Hans soon began to take a prominent place. His parents were both among my closest adherents, and they had agreed that in bringing up their first child they would use no more coercion than might be absolutely necessary for maintaining good behaviour. And, as the child developed into a cheerful, good-natured, and lively little boy, the experiment of letting him grow up and express himself without being intimidated went on satisfactorily. I shall now proceed to reproduce his father's records of little Hans just as I received them; and I shall of course refrain from any attempt at spoiling the *naïveté* and directness of the nursery by making any conventional emendations.

The first reports of Hans date from a period when he was not quite three years old. At that time, by means of various remarks and questions, he was showing a quite peculiarly lively interest in that portion of his body which he used to describe as his "widdler."[2] Thus he once asked his mother this question:

Hans: "Mamma, have you got a widdler too?"
Mother: "Of course. Why?"
Hans: "I was only just thinking."

At the same age he went into a cow-shed once and saw a cow being milked. "Oh, look!" he said, "there's milk coming out of its widdler!"

Even these first observations begin to rouse an expectation that much, if not most, of what little Hans shows us will turn out to be typical for the sexual development of children in general. I once put forward the view[3] that there was no need to be too much horrified at finding in a woman the idea of sucking at the male organ. This repulsive propensity, I argued, had a most innocent origin, since it was derived from sucking at the mother's breast; and in this connection, I went on, the udder of a cow plays an apt part as an intermediate image, being in its nature a mamma and in its shape and position a penis. Little Hans's discovery confirms the latter part of my contention.

Meanwhile his interest in widdlers was by no means a purely theoretical one; as might have been expected, it impelled him to touch his member. When he was three and a half his mother found him with his hand to his penis. She threatened him in these words: "If you do that, I shall send for Dr. A. to cut off your widdler. And then what'll you widdle with?"

Hans: "With my bottom."

He made this reply without having any sense of guilt as yet. But this was the occasion of his acquiring the "castra-

[2] [*"Wiwimacher"* in the original.—*Trans.*]
[3] "Fragment of an Analysis of a Case of Hysteria." (See *Dora—An Analysis of a Case of Hysteria,* Collier Books edition AS 581V.)

tion complex," the presence of which we are so often obliged to infer in analysing neurotics, though they one and all struggle violently against recognizing it. There is much of importance to be said upon the significance of this element in the life of a child. The "castration complex" has left marked traces behind it in myths (and not only in Greek myths); in a passage in my *Traumdeutung*,[4] and elsewhere, I have touched upon the part it plays.[5]

At about the same age (three and a half), standing in front of the lions' cage at Schönbrunn,[6] little Hans called

[4] Seventh Edition, p. 456.

[5] (*Additional Note, 1923.*)—Since this was written, the study of the castration complex has been further developed in contributions to the subject by Lou Andreas, A. Stärcke, F. Alexander, and others. It has been urged that every time his mother's breast is withdrawn from a baby he is bound to feel it as castration (that is to say, as the loss of what he regards as an important part of his own body); that, further, he cannot fail to be similarly affected by the regular loss of his faeces; and, finally, that the act of birth itself (consisting as it does of the separation of the child from his mother, with whom he has hitherto been united) is the prototype of all castration. While recognizing all of these roots of the complex, I have nevertheless put forward the view that the term "castration complex" ought to be confined to those excitations and effects which are bound up with the loss of the penis. Any one who, in analysing adults, has become convinced of the invariable presence of the castration complex, will of course find difficulty in ascribing its origin to a chance threat—of a kind which is not, after all, of such universal occurrence; he will be driven to assume that the child constructs this danger for itself out of the slightest hints, which will never be wanting. This circumstance is also the motive, indeed, that has stimulated the search for those deeper roots of the complex which are universally forthcoming. But this makes it all the more valuable that in the case of little Hans the threat of castration is reported by his parents themselves, and moreover at a date before there was any question of his phobia.

[6] [The imperial palace on the outskirts of Vienna. There is a zoological collection in the park.—*Trans.*]

out in a joyful and excited voice: "I saw the lion's widdler."

Animals owe a good deal of their importance in myths and fairy tales to the openness with which they display their genitals and their sexual functions to the inquisitive little human child. There can be no doubt as to the existence of Hans's sexual curiosity; but it roused the spirit of inquiry in him and enabled him to arrive at genuine abstract knowledge.

When he was at the station once (at three and three-quarters) he saw some water being let out of an engine. "Oh, look," he said, "the engine's widdling. Where's it got its widdler?"

After a little he added in reflective tones: "A dog and a horse have widdlers; a table and a chair haven't." He had thus got hold of an essential characteristic for differentiating between animate and inanimate objects.

Thirst for knowledge seems to be inseparable from sexual curiosity. Hans's curiosity was particularly directed towards his parents.

Hans (aged three and three-quarters): "Papa, have you got a widdler too?"

Father: "Yes, of course."

Hans: "But I've never seen it when you were undressing."

Another time he was looking on intently while his mother undressed before going to bed. "What are you staring like that for?" she asked.

Hans: "I was only looking to see if you'd got a widdler too."

Mother: "Of course. Didn't you know that?"

Hans: "No. I thought you were so big you'd have a widdler like a horse."

This expectation of little Hans's deserves to be noted; it will become important later on.

But the great event of Hans's life was the birth of his little sister Hanna when he was exactly three and a half.[7] His behaviour on that occasion was noted down by his father on the spot: "At five in the morning," he writes, "labour began, and Hans's bed was moved into the next room. He woke up there at seven, and hearing his mother groaning, asked: 'Why's mamma coughing?' Then, after a pause, 'The stork's coming to-day for certain.'

"Naturally he has often been told during the last few days that the stork is going to bring a little girl or a little boy; and he quite rightly connected the unusual sounds of groaning with the stork's arrival.

"Later on he was taken into the kitchen. He saw the doctor's bag in the front hall and asked: 'What's that?' 'A bag,' was the reply. Upon which he declared with conviction: 'The stork's coming today.' After the delivery of the child the midwife came into the kitchen and Hans heard her ordering some tea to be made. At this he said: 'I know! Mummy's to have some tea because she's coughing.' He was then called into the bedroom. He did not look at his mother, however, but at the basins and other vessels, filled with blood and water, that were still standing about the room. Pointing to the blood-stained bedpan, he observed in a surprised voice: 'But blood doesn't come out of *my* widdler.'

"Everything he says shows that he connects what is strange in the situation with the arrival of the stork. He meets everything he sees with a very suspicious and intent look, and *there can be no doubt that his first suspicions about the stork have made their appearance*.

"Hans is very jealous of the new arrival, and whenever any one praises her, says she is a lovely baby, and so on, he at once declares scornfully: 'But she hasn't got any teeth yet.'[8] And in fact when he saw her for the first time

---

[7] April 1903 to October 1906.

[8] This again is a typical mode of behaviour. Another little boy, only two years his sister's senior, used to parry similar remarks with an angry cry of "Too 'ickle! too 'ickle!"

he was very much surprised that she could not speak, and decided that this was because she had no teeth. During the first few days he was naturally put very much in the background. He was suddenly taken ill with a sore throat. In his fever he was heard saying: 'But I don't want a little sister!'

"Some six months later he had got over his jealousy, and his brotherly affection for the baby was only equalled by his sense of his own superiority over her.[9]

"A week later Hans was watching his seven-day-old sister being given a bath. 'But her widdler's still quite small,' he remarked; and then added, as though by way of consolation: 'When she grows up it'll get bigger all right.'[10]

[9] Another child, rather older than Hans, welcomed his younger brother with the words: "The stork must take him away again." Compare with this my remarks in *Traumdeutung* upon the dreams of the death of dear relatives (Seventh Edition, pp. 171 ff.).

[10] Two other boys were reported to me as having made the same judgement, expressed in identical words and followed by the same anticipation, when they were allowed to satisfy their curiosity and look at their baby sister's body for the first time. One might well feel horrified at such signs of the premature ruin of a child's intellect. Why did not these young inquirers state what they really saw, namely, that there was no widdler there? In little Hans's case, at all events, we can account completely for the faulty perception. We are aware that by a process of careful induction he had arrived at the general proposition that every animate object, in contradistinction to inanimate ones, possesses a widdler. His mother had confirmed him in this conviction by giving him corroborative information in regard to persons inaccessible to his own observation. He was now utterly incapable of surrendering what he had achieved merely on the strength of this single observation made upon his little sister. He therefore made a judgement that in that instance also there was a widdler present, only that it was still very small, but that it would grow till it was as big as a horse's.

We can go a step further in vindicating little Hans's honour.

"At the same age (when he was three and three-quarters) Hans produced his first account of a dream: 'To-day when I was asleep I thought I was at Gmunden[11] with Mariedl.'

"Mariedl was the thirteen-year-old daughter of our landlord and used often to play with him."

As Hans's father was telling his mother the dream in his presence, he corrected him, saying: "Not with Mariedl, but quite alone with Mariedl."

In this connection we learn: "In the summer of 1906 Hans was at Gmunden, and used to run about all day long with our landlord's children. When we left Gmunden we thought he would be very much upset by having to come away and move into town. To our surprise this was not so. He seemed glad at the change, and for several weeks he talked very little about Gmunden. It was not until after

---

As a matter of fact, he behaved no worse than a philosopher of the school of Wundt. In the view of that school, consciousness is the invariable characteristic of what is mental, just as in the view of little Hans a widdler is the indispensable criterion of what is animate. If now the philosopher comes across mental processes, the existence of which has to be inferred, but about which there is not a trace of consciousness to be detected—for the subject, in fact, knows nothing of them, although it is impossible to avoid inferring their existence—then, instead of saying that they are *un*conscious mental processes, he calls them *semi*-conscious. The widdler is still very small! And in this comparison the advantage is in favour of little Hans. For, as is so often the case with the sexual inquiries of children, behind the mistake a piece of genuine knowledge lies concealed. Little girls do possess a small widdler, which we call a clitoris, though it does not grow any larger but remains permanently stunted. (Compare my short paper "On the Sexual Theories of Children," *supra*.)

[11] [A summer resort on one of the Austrian lakes.—Mariedl, Franzl, Fritzl, and similar forms are the characteristically Austrian affectionate diminutives of Marie, Franz, Fritz, etc. —*Trans.*]

some weeks had passed that there began to emerge reminiscences—often vividly coloured—of the time he had
spent at Gmunden. During the last four weeks or so he
has been working these reminiscences up into phantasies.
He imagines that he is playing with the other children,
with Berta, Olga, and Fritzl; he talks to them as though
they were really with him, and he is capable of amusing
himself in this way for hours at a time. Now that he has
got a sister and is obviously taken up with the problem of
the origin of children, he always calls Berta and Olga 'his
children'; and once he added: 'my children Berta and Olga
were brought by the stork too.' The dream, occurring now,
after six months' absence from Gmunden, is evidently to
be read as an expression of a longing to go back there."

Thus far his father. I will anticipate what is to come by
adding that when Hans made this last remark about his
children having been brought by the stork, he was contradicting aloud a doubt that was lurking within him.

His father luckily made a note of many things which
turned out later on to be of unexpected value. "I drew a
giraffe for Hans, who has been to Schönbrunn several
times lately. He said to me: 'Draw its widdler too.' 'Draw
it yourself,' I answered; whereupon he added this line to
my picture (see Fig. 1). He began by drawing a short

Fig. 1

stroke, and then added a bit on to it, remarking: 'Its widdler's longer.'

"Hans and I walked past a horse that was urinating, and he said: 'The horse has got its widdler underneath like me.'

"He was watching his three-months-old sister being given a bath, and said in pitying tones: 'She *has* got a tiny little widdler.'

"He was given a doll to play with and undressed it. He examined it carefully and said: 'Her widdler's ever so tiny.'"

As we already know, this formula made it possible for him to go on believing in his discovery (see p. 53).

Every investigator runs the risk of falling into an occasional error. It is some consolation for him if, like little Hans in the next example, he does not err alone but can quote a common usage of language in his support. For Hans saw a monkey in his picture-book one day, and pointing to its up-curled tail, said: "Daddy, look at its widdler!"

His interest in widdlers led him to invent a special game of his own. "Leading out of the front hall there is a lavatory and also a dark storeroom for keeping wood in. For some time past Hans has been going into this wood-cupboard and saying: 'I'm going to my W.C.' I once looked in to see what he was doing in the dark storeroom. He showed me his parts and said: 'I'm widdling.' That is to say, he has been 'playing' at W.C. That it is in the nature of a game is shown not merely by the fact that he was only pretending to widdle, but also by the fact that he does not go into the W.C., which would after all be far simpler, but prefers the wood-cupboard and calls it 'his W.C.'"

We should be doing Hans an injustice if we were to trace only the auto-erotic features of his sexual life. His father has detailed information to give us on the subject of his love relationships with other children. From these we can discern the existence of an "object-choice" just as in the case of an adult; and also, it must be confessed, a very striking degree of inconstancy and a disposition to polygamy.

"In the winter (at the age of three and three-quarters) I took Hans to the Skating Rink and introduced him to my friend N.'s two little daughters, who were about ten years old. Hans sat down beside them, while they, in the consciousness of their mature age, looked down on the little urchin with a good deal of contempt; he gazed at them with admiration, though this proceeding made no great impression on them. In spite of this Hans always spoke of them afterwards as 'my little girls.' 'Where are my little girls? When are my little girls coming?' And for some weeks he kept tormenting me with the question: 'When am I going to the Rink again to see my little girls?' "

A five-year-old boy cousin came to visit Hans, who had by then reached the age of four. Hans was constantly putting his arms round him, and once, as he was giving him one of these tender embraces, said: "I *am* so fond of you."

This is the first trace of homosexuality that we have come across in him, but it will not be the last. Little Hans seems to be a positive paragon of all the vices.

"When Hans was four years old we moved into a new flat. A door led out of the kitchen on to a balcony, from which one could see into a flat on the opposite side of the courtyard. In this flat Hans discovered a little girl of about seven or eight. He would sit on the step leading on to the balcony so as to admire her, and would stop there for hours on end. At four o'clock in the afternoon in particular, when the little girl came home from school, he was not to be kept in the room, and nothing could induce him to abandon his post of observation. Once, when the little girl failed to make her appearance at the window at her usual hour, Hans grew quite restless, and kept pestering the servants with questions—'When's the little girl coming? Where's the little girl?' and so on. When she did appear at last, he was quite blissful and never took his eyes off the flat opposite. The violence with which this 'long-range love'[12] came over him is to be explained by his having no playfellows of either sex. Spending a great deal of time with other children clearly enters into a child's normal development.

"Hans obtained some companionship of this kind when, shortly afterwards (he was by then four and a half), we moved to Gmunden for the summer holidays. In our house there his playmates were our landlord's children: Franzl (about twelve years old), Fritzl (eight), Olga (seven), and Berta (five). Besides these there were the neighbour's children, Anna (ten), and two other little girls of nine and seven whose names I have forgotten. Hans's favourite was Fritzl; he often hugged him and made protestations of his love. Once when he was asked: 'Which of the girls are you fondest of?' he answered: 'Fritzl!' At the same time he treated the girls in a most aggressive, masculine and arrogant way, embracing them and kissing them heartily—a process to which Berta in particular offered no objection. When Berta was coming out of the room one evening he put his arm round her neck and said in the fondest tones: 'Berta, you *are* a dear!' This, by the way, did not prevent his kissing the others as well and assuring them of his love. He was fond, too, of the fourteen-year-old Mariedl— another of our landlord's daughters—who used to play with him. One evening as he was being put to bed he said: 'I want Mariedl to sleep with me.' On being told that would not do, he said: 'Then she shall sleep with Mummy or with Daddy.' He was told that would not do either, but that Mariedl must sleep with her own father and mother. Upon which the following dialogue took place:

Hans: "Oh, then I'll just go downstairs and sleep with Mariedl."

---

[12] "Und die Liebe per Distanz,
    Kurzgesagt, missfällt mir ganz."
                                    —Wilhelm Busch.
    ["Long-range love, I must admit,
    Does not suit my taste a bit."]

Mother: "You really want to go away from Mummy and sleep downstairs?"

Hans: "Oh, I'll come up again in the morning to have breakfast and do number one."

Mother: "Well, if you really want to go away from Daddy and Mummy, then take your coat and knickers and—good-bye!"

"Hans did in fact take his clothes and go towards the staircase, to go and sleep with Mariedl, but, it need hardly be said, he was fetched back."

"(Behind his wish, 'I want Mariedl to sleep with us,' there lay another one: 'I want Mariedl' (with whom he liked to be so much) 'to become one of our family.' But Hans's father and mother were in the habit of taking him into their bed, though only occasionally, and there can be no doubt that lying beside them had aroused erotic feelings in him; so that his wish to sleep with Mariedl had an erotic sense as well. Lying in bed with his father or mother was a source of erotic feelings in Hans just as it is in every other child.)"

In spite of his accesses of homosexuality, little Hans bore himself like a true man in the face of his mother's challenge.

"In the next instance, too, Hans said to his mother: 'I say, I *should* so like to sleep with the little girl.'"

This episode has given us a great deal of entertainment, for Hans has really behaved like a grown-up person in love. For the last few days a pretty little girl of about eight has been coming to the restaurant where we have lunch. Of course Hans fell in love with her on the spot. He keeps constantly turning round in his chair to take furtive looks at her; when he has finished eating he stations himself in her vicinity so as to flirt with her, but if he finds he is being observed, he blushes scarlet. If his glances are returned by the little girl, he at once looks shamefacedly the other way. His behaviour is naturally a great joy to every one lunching at the restaurant. Every day as he is taken there he says: 'Do you think the little girl will be there to-day?' And when at last she appears, he goes quite red, just as a grown-up person would in such a case. One day he came to me with a beaming face and whispered in my ear: 'Daddy, I know where the little girl lives. I saw her going up the steps in such-and-such a place.' Whereas he treats the little girls at home aggressively, in this other affair he appears in the part of a platonic and languishing admirer. Perhaps this has to do with the little girls at home being village children, while the other is a young lady of refinement. As I have already mentioned, he once said he would like to sleep with her.

"Not wanting Hans to be left in the overwrought state to which he had been brought by his passion for the little girl, I managed to make them acquainted, and invited the little girl to come and see him in the garden after he had finished his afternoon sleep. Hans was so much excited at the prospect of the little girl coming, that for the first time he could not get off to sleep in the afternoon, but tossed about restlessly on his bed. When his mother asked, 'Why aren't you asleep? Are you thinking about the little girl?' he said 'Yes' with a happy look. And when he came home from the restaurant he said to every one in the house: 'I say, my little girl's coming to see me to-day.' The fourteen-year-old Mariedl reported that he had repeatedly kept asking her: 'I say, do you think she'll be nice to me? Do you think she'll kiss me if I kiss her?' and so on.

"But in the afternoon it rained, so that the visit did not come off, and Hans consoled himself with Berta and Olga."

Other observations, also made at the time of the summer holidays, suggest that all sorts of new developments were going on in the little boy.

"Hans, four and a quarter. This morning Hans was given his usual daily bath by his mother and afterwards dried and powdered. As his mother was powdering round his penis and taking care not to touch it, Hans said: 'Why don't you put your finger there?'

Mother: "Because that'd be piggish."

Hans: "What's that? Piggish? Why?"
Mother: "Because it's not proper."
Hans: (laughing): "But it's great fun."[13]

At about the same period Hans had a dream which was in striking contrast with the boldness he had shown towards his mother. It was the first dream of his that was made unrecognizable by distortion. His father's penetration, however, succeeded in clearing it up.

"Hans, four and a quarter. *Dream.* This morning Hans woke up and said: 'I say, last night I thought: *Some one said: "Who wants to come to me?" Then some one said: "I do." Then he had to make him widdle.*'

"Further questions made it clear that there was no visual content whatever in this dream, and that it was of the purely auditory type. During the last few days Hans has been playing parlour games and forfeits with our landlord's children, amongst whom are his friends Olga (aged seven) and Berta (aged five). (The game of forfeits is played in this way: *A:* 'Whose is this forfeit in my hand?' *B:* 'Mine.' Then it is decided what *B* must do.) The dream is modelled upon this game; only Hans wishes that the person to whom the forfeit belonged shall be condemned, not to give the usual kiss or be given the usual box on the ear, but to widdle, or rather to make some one else widdle.

"I got him to tell me the dream again. He told it in the same words, except that instead of 'then some one said' this time he said 'then she said.' This 'she' is obviously Berta or Olga, one of the girls he had been playing with. Translated, the dream runs as follows: 'I was playing forfeits with the little girls. I asked: "Who wants to come to

---

[13] Another mother, a neurotic, who would not believe in infantile masturbation, told me of a similar attempt at seduction on the part of her three-and-a-half-year-old daughter. She had had a pair of drawers made for the little girl, and was trying them on her to see whether they were not too tight for walking. To do this she passed her hands upwards along the inner surface of the child's thigh. Suddenly the little girl shut her legs together on her mother's hand, saying: "Oh, Mummy, *do* leave your hand there. It feels so lovely."

me?" She (Berta or Olga) replied: "I do." Then she had to make me widdle.' (That is, she had to assist him in urinating, which is evidently agreeable for Hans.)

"It is clear that being made to widdle—having his knickers unbuttoned and his penis taken out—is a pleasurable process for Hans. On walks it is mostly his father who assists Hans in this way; and this gives the child an opportunity for the fixation of homosexual inclinations upon him.

"Two days ago, as I have already reported, while his mother was washing and powdering his genital region, he asked her: 'Why don't you put your finger there?' Yesterday, when I was helping Hans to do number one, he asked me for the first time to take him to the back of the house so that no one should see him. He added: 'Last year when I widdled, Berta and Olga watched me.' This meant, I think, that last year he had enjoyed being watched by the girls, but that this was no longer so. His exhibitionism has now succumbed to repression. The fact that the wish that Berta and Olga should watch him widdling (or make him widdle) is now repressed in real life is the explanation of its appearance in the dream, where it was prettily disguised under the game of forfeits.—I have repeatedly observed since then that he does not like to be seen widdling."

I will only add that this dream obeys the rule I have given in *Traumdeutung*[14] to the effect that speeches occurring in dreams are derived from speeches heard or spoken by the dreamer during the preceding days.

Hans's father has noted down one other observation, dating from the period immediately after their return to Vienna: "Hans (aged four and a half) was again watching his little sister being given her bath, when he began laughing. On being asked why he was laughing, he replied: 'I'm laughing at Hanna's widdler.' 'Why?' 'Because her widdler's so lovely.'

"Of course his answer was a disingenuous one. In

---

[14] Seventh Edition, pp. 283 *et seq*.

reality her widdler had seemed to him funny. Moreover, this is the first time he has recognized in this way the distinction between male and female genitals instead of denying it."

2. Case History and Analysis

"My dear Professor, I am sending you a little more about Hans—but this time, I am sorry to say, material for a case history. As you will see, during the last few days he has developed a nervous disorder, which has made my wife and me most uneasy, because we have not been able to find any means of dissipating it. I shall venture to call upon you to-morrow, . . . but in the meantime . . . I enclose a written record of the material available.

"No doubt the ground was prepared by sexual over-excitation due to his mother's tenderness; but I am not able to specify the actual exciting cause. He is afraid *that a horse will bite him in the street,* and this fear seems somehow to be connected with his having been frightened by a large penis. As you know from a former report, he had noticed at a very early age what large penises horses have, and at that time he inferred that as his mother was so large she must have a widdler like a horse.

"I cannot see what to make of it. Has he seen an exhibitionist somewhere? Or is the whole thing simply connected with his mother? It is not very pleasant for us that he should begin setting us problems so early. Apart from his being afraid of going into the street and from his being depressed in the evening, he is in other respects the same Hans, as bright and cheerful as ever."

We will not follow Hans's father either in his easily comprehensible anxieties or in his first attempts at finding an explanation; we will begin by examining the material before us. It is not in the least our business to "understand" a case at once; this is only possible at a later stage, when we have received enough impressions of it. For the present we will suspend our judgement and give our impartial attention to everything that there is to observe.

The earliest accounts, dating from the first days in January of the present year (1908), run as follows:

"Hans (aged four and three-quarters) woke up one morning in tears. Asked why he was crying, he said to his mother: 'When I was asleep I thought you were gone and I had no Mummy to coax with.'[1]

"An anxiety dream, therefore.

"I had already noticed something similar at Gmunden in the summer. When he was in bed in the evening he was usually in a very sentimental state. Once he made a remark to this effect: 'Suppose I was to have no Mummy,' or 'Suppose you were to go away,' or something of the sort; I cannot remember the exact words. Unfortunately, when he got into an elegiac mood of that kind, his mother used always to take him into bed with her.

"On about January 5th he came into his mother's bed in the morning, and said: 'Do you know what Aunt M. said? She said: "He *has* got a dear little thingummy." '[2] (Aunt M. was stopping with us four weeks ago. Once while she was watching my wife giving the boy a bath she did in fact say these words to her in a low voice. Hans had overheard them and was now trying to put them to his own uses.)

"On January 7th he went to the Stadtpark[3] with his nursemaid as usual. In the street he began to cry and asked to be taken home, saying that he wanted to 'coax' with his Mummy. At home he was asked why he had refused to go any farther and had cried, but he would not say. Till the evening he was cheerful, as usual. But in the evening he grew visibly frightened; he cried and could not

[1] "Hans's expression for 'to caress.' "

[2] Meaning his penis. It is one of the commonest things—psychoanalyses are full of such incidents—for children's genitals to be caressed, not only in word but in deed, by fond relations, including even parents themselves.

[3] [Public gardens near the centre of Vienna.—*Trans.*]

be separated from his mother, and wanted to 'coax' with her again. Then he grew cheerful again, and slept well.

"On January 8th my wife decided to go out with him herself, so as to see what was wrong with him. They went to Schönbrunn, where he always likes going. Again he began to cry, did not want to start, and was frightened. In the end he did go; but was visibly frightened in the street. On the way back from Schönbrunn he said to his mother, after much internal struggling: *'I was afraid a horse would bite me.'* (He had, in fact, become uneasy at Schönbrunn when he saw a horse.) In the evening he seems to have had another attack similar to that of the previous evening, and to have wanted to be 'coaxed' with. He was calmed down. He said, crying. 'I know I shall have to go for a walk again to-morrow.' And later: 'The horse 'll come into the room.'

"On the same day his mother asked: 'Do you put your hand to your widdler?' and he answered: 'Yes. Every evening, when I'm in bed.' The next day, January 9th, he was warned, before his afternoon sleep, not to put his hand to his widdler. When he woke up he was asked about it, and said he had put it there for a short while all the same."

Here, then, we have the beginning of Hans's morbid anxiety as well as of his phobia. As we see, there is good reason for keeping the two separate. Moreover, the material seems to be amply sufficient for giving us our bearings; and no moment of time is so favourable for the understanding of a case as its initial stage, such as we have here, though unluckily that stage is as a rule neglected or passed over in silence. The disorder set in with thoughts that were at the same time fearful and sentimental, and then followed an anxiety dream on the subject of losing his mother and so not being able to coax with her any more. His affection for his mother must therefore have become enormously intensified. This was the fundamental phenomenon in his condition. In support of this, we may recall his two attempts at seducing his mother, the first of which dated back to the summer, while the second (a simple commendation of his penis) occurred immediately before the outbreak of his street-phobia. It was this increased affection for his mother which turned suddenly into anxiety—which, as we should say, succumbed to repression. We do not yet know from what quarter the impetus towards repression may have come. Perhaps it was merely the result of the intensity of the child's emotions, which had become greater than it could control; or perhaps other forces which we have not yet recognized were also at work. This we shall learn as we go on. Hans's anxiety, which thus corresponded to a repressed erotic longing, was, like every infantile anxiety, without an object to begin with: it was still anxiety and not yet fear. The child cannot tell what it is afraid of; and when Hans, on the first walk with the nursemaid, would not say what he was afraid of, it was simply that he himself did not yet know. He said all that he knew, which was that in the street he missed his mother, whom he could coax with, and that he did not want to be away from her. In saying this he quite straightforwardly confessed the primary meaning of his dislike of streets.

Then again, there were the states into which he fell on two consecutive evenings before going to sleep, and which were characterized by anxiety mingled with clear traces of tenderness. These states show that at the beginning of his illness there was as yet no phobia whatever present, whether of streets or of walking or even of horses. If there had been, his evening states would be inexplicable; for who bothers at bedtime about streets and walking? On the other hand it becomes quite clear why he was so fearful in the evening, if we suppose that at bedtime he was overwhelmed by an intensification of his libido—for its object was his mother, and its aim may perhaps have been to sleep with her. He had besides learnt from his experience that *at Gmunden* his mother could be prevailed upon, when he got into such moods, to take him into her bed, and he wanted to gain the same ends here in Vienna. Nor must we forget that for part of the time at Gmunden he had been alone with his mother, as his father had not been able to spend the whole of the holidays there; and further, that in the country his affections had been divided among a number of playmates and friends of both sexes, while in Vienna he had none, so that his libido was in a position to return undivided to his mother.

His morbid anxiety, then, corresponded to repressed longing. But it was not the same thing as the longing: the repression must be taken into account too. Longing can be completely transformed into satisfaction if it is presented with the object longed for. Therapy of that kind is no longer effective in dealing with anxiety. The anxiety remains even when the longing can be satisfied. It can no longer be completely retransformed into libido; there is something that keeps the libido back under repression.[4] This was shown to be so in the case of Hans on the occasion of his next walk, when his mother went with him. He was with his mother, and yet he still suffered from anxiety —that is to say, from an unsatisfied longing for her. It is true that the anxiety was less; for he did allow himself to be induced to go for the walk, whereas he had obliged the nursemaid to turn back. Nor is a street quite the right place for "coaxing," or whatever else this young lover may have wanted. But his anxiety had stood the test; and the next thing for it to do was to find an object. It was on this walk that he first expressed a fear that a horse would bite him. Where did the material for this phobia come from? Probably from the complexes, as yet unknown to us, which had contributed to the repression and were keeping under repression his libidinal feelings towards his mother. That is an unsolved problem, and we shall now have to follow the development of the case in order to arrive at its solution. Hans's father has already given us certain clues,

[4] To speak quite frankly, this is actually the criterion according to which we decide whether such feelings of mingled apprehension and longing are normal or not: we begin to call them "pathological anxiety" from the moment at which they can no longer be relieved by the attainment of the object longed for.

probably trustworthy ones, such as that Hans had always observed horses with interest on account of their large widdlers, that he had supposed that his mother must have a widdler like a horse, and so on. We might thus be led to think that the horse was merely a substitute for his mother. But if so, what would be the meaning of his being afraid in the evening that a horse would come into the room? A small boy's foolish fears, it will be said. But a neurosis never says foolish things, any more than a dream. When we cannot understand something, we always fall back on abuse. An excellent way of making a task lighter.

There is another point in regard to which we must avoid giving way to this temptation. Hans admitted that every night before going to sleep he amused himself with playing with his penis. "Ah!" the family doctor will be inclined to say, "now we have it. The child masturbated: hence its pathological anxiety." But gently. That the child was getting pleasure for itself by masturbating does not by any means explain its anxiety; on the contrary, it makes it more problematical than ever. States of anxiety are not produced by masturbation or by getting satisfaction in any shape. Moreover, we may presume that Hans, who was now four and three-quarters, had been indulging in this pleasure every evening for at least a year (see p. 49). And we shall find that at this moment he was actually engaged in a struggle to break himself of the habit—a state of things which fits in much better with repression and anxiety-formation.

We must say a word, too, on behalf of Hans's excellent and devoted mother. His father accuses her, not without some show of justice, of being responsible for the outbreak of the child's neurosis, on account of her excessive display of affection for him and her too frequent readiness to take him into her bed. We might as easily blame her for having precipitated the process of repression by her energetic rejection of his advances ("that'd be piggish"). But she had a predestined part to play, and her position was a hard one.

I arranged with Hans's father that he should tell the

boy that all this business about horses was a piece of nonsense and nothing more. The truth was, his father was to say, that he was very fond of his mother and wanted to be taken into her bed. The reason he was afraid of horses now was that he had taken so much interest in their widdlers. He himself had noticed that it was not right to be so very much preoccupied with widdlers, even with his own, and he was quite right in thinking this. I further suggested to his father that he should begin giving Hans some enlightenment in the matter of sex knowledge. The child's past behaviour justified us in assuming that his libido was attached to a wish to see his mother's widdler; so I proposed to his father that he should take away this aim from Hans by informing him that his mother and all other female beings (as he could see from Hanna) had no widdler at all. This last piece of enlightenment was to be given him on a suitable occasion when it had been led up to by some question or some chance remark on Hans's part.

The next batch of news about Hans covers the period from March 1st to March 17th. The interval of more than a month will be accounted for directly.

"After Hans had been enlightened,[5] there followed a fairly quiet period, during which he could be induced without any particular difficulty to go for his daily walk in the Stadtpark. His fear of horses became transformed more and more into an obsession for looking at them. He said: 'I have to look at horses, and then I'm frightened.'

"After an attack of influenza, which kept him in bed for two weeks, his phobia increased again so much that he could not be induced to go out, or at most on to the balcony. Every Sunday he went with me to Lainz,[6] because on that day there is not much traffic in the streets, and it

[5] As to the meaning of his anxiety; not yet as to women having no widdlers.

[6] A suburb of Vienna [not far from Schönbrunn] where Hans's grandparents lived.

is only a short way to the station. On that occasion in Lainz he refused to go for a walk outside the garden because there was a carriage standing in front of it. After another week which he has had to spend indoors because he has had his tonsils cut, the phobia has grown very much worse again. He goes out on to the balcony, it is true, but not for a walk. As soon as he gets to the street door he hurriedly turns round.

"On Sunday, March 1st, the following conversation took place on the way to the station. I was once more trying to explain to him that horses do not bite. *He:* 'But white horses bite. There's a white horse at Gmunden that bites. If you hold your finger to it it bites.' (I was struck by his saying 'finger' instead of 'hand.') He then told me the following story, which I give here in a connected form: 'When Lizzi had to go away, there was a cart with a white horse in front of her house, to take her luggage to the station.' (Lizzi, he tells me, was a little girl who lived in a neighbouring house.) 'Her father was standing near the horse, and the horse turned its head round (to touch him), and he said to Lizzi: *"Don't put your finger to the white horse or it'll bite you."* ' Upon this I said: 'I say, it strikes me that it isn't a horse you mean, but a widdler, that one mustn't put one's hand to.'

He: "But a widdler doesn't bite."

I: "Perhaps it does, though." He then went on eagerly to try and prove to me that it really was a white horse.[7]

"On March 2nd, as he again showed signs of being afraid, I said to him: 'Do you know what? This nonsense of yours' (that is how he speaks of his phobia) 'will get better if you go for more walks. It's so bad now because you haven't been able to go out because you were ill.'

---

[7] Hans's father had no reason to doubt that it was a real event that the boy was describing.—I may also mention that the sensations of itching in the glans penis, which lead children to touch their genitals, are usually described by them in the phrase "Es beisst mich" ["I'm itching," literally "it bites me"].

He: "Oh no, it's so bad because I still put my hand to my widdler every night."

Doctor and patient, father and son, were therefore at one in ascribing the chief share in the pathogenesis of Hans's present condition to his habit of onanism. Signs were not wanting, however, of the presence of other significant factors.

"On March 3rd we got in a new maid, whom he is particularly pleased with. She lets him ride on her back while she cleans the floor, and so he always calls her 'my horse,' and holds on to her dress with cries of 'Gee-up.' On about March 10th he said to this new nursemaid: 'If you do such-and-such a thing you'll have to undress altogether, and take off your chemise even.' " (He meant this as a punishment, but it is easy to recognize the wish behind it.)

She: "And what'd be the harm? I'd just say to myself I haven't got any money to spend on clothes."

He: "Why, it'd be shameful. People'd see your widdler."

Here we have the same curiosity again, but directed on to a new object, and (appropriately to a time of repression) cloaked under a moralizing purpose.

"On March 13th in the morning I said to Hans: 'You know, if you don't put your hand to your widdler any more, this nonsense of yours 'll soon get better.'

Hans: "But I don't put my hand to my widdler any more."

I: "But you still want to."

Hans: "Yes, I do. But wanting's not doing, and doing's not wanting." (!!)

I: "Well, but to prevent your wanting to, this evening you're going to have a sack to sleep in."

"After this we went out in front of the house. Hans was still afraid, but his spirits were visibly raised by the prospect of having his struggles made easier for him, and he said: 'Oh, if I have a sack to sleep in my nonsense 'll have gone to-morrow.' And, in fact, he was *much* less afraid of horses, and was fairly calm when vehicles drove past.

"Hans had promised to go with me to Lainz the next Sunday, March 15th. He resisted at first, but finally went with me all the same. He obviously felt all right in the street, as there was not much traffic, and said: 'How sensible! God's done away with horses now.' On the way I explained to him that his sister has not got a widdler like him. Little girls and women, I said, have no widdlers: Mummy has none, Anna has none, and so on.

Hans: "Have you got a widdler?"

I: "Of course. Why, what do you suppose?"

Hans (after a pause): "But how do little girls widdle, if they have no widdlers?"

I: "They don't have widdlers like yours. Haven't you noticed already, when Hanna was being given her bath?"

"All day long he was in very high spirits, went tobogganing, and so on. It was only towards evening that he became depressed again and seemed to be afraid of horses.

"That evening the nervous attack and the need for being coaxed with was less pronounced than on former days. Next day his mother took him with her into town and he was very much frightened in the streets. The day after, he stopped at home and was very cheerful. Next morning he woke up in a fright at about six o'clock. When he was asked what was the matter he said: 'I put my finger to my widdler just a very little. I saw Mummy quite naked in her chemise, and she let me see her widdler. I showed Grete,[8] my Grete, what Mamma was doing, and showed her my widdler. Then I took my hand away from my widdler quick.' When I objected that he could only mean 'in her chemise' *or* 'quite naked,' Hans said: 'She was in her

_____

[8] "Grete is one of the little girls at Gmunden about whom Hans is having phantasies just now; he talks and plays with her."

chemise, but the chemise was so short that I saw her widdler.' "

This was none of it a dream, but an onanistic phantasy, which was, however, equivalent to a dream. What he made his mother do was evidently intended as a piece of self-justification: "If Mummy shows her widdler, I may too."

We can gather two things from this phantasy: first, that his mother's reproof had exercised a powerful effect upon him at the time it was made, and secondly, that the enlightenment he had been given to the effect that women have no widdlers was not accepted by him at first. He regretted that it should be so, and stuck to his former view in his phantasy. He may also perhaps have had his reasons for refusing to believe his father at first.

Weekly Report from Hans's Father: "My dear Professor, I enclose the continuation of Hans's story—quite an interesting instalment. I shall perhaps take the liberty of calling upon you during your consulting hours on Monday and if possible of bringing Hans with me—assuming that he will come. I said to him to-day: 'Will you come with me on Monday to see the Professor, who can take away your nonsense for you?'

He: "No."

I: "But he's got a very pretty little girl."—Upon which he willingly and gladly consented.

"Sunday, March 22nd. With a view to extending the Sunday programme, I proposed to Hans that we should go first to Schönbrunn, and only go on from there to Lainz at midday. He had, therefore, to make his way not only from our house to the Hauptzollamt station on the Stadtbahn,[9] but also from the Hietzing station to Schönbrunn, and again from there to the Hietzing steam tramway station. And he managed all this, looking hurriedly away whenever

[9] [The Head Customs House station on the Vienna local and suburban railway. Hietzing is a suburb which adjoins the palace of Schönbrunn.—*Trans.*]

any horses came along, for he was evidently feeling nervous. In looking away he was following a piece of advice given him by his mother.

"At Schönbrunn he showed signs of fear at animals which on other occasions he had looked at without any alarm. Thus he absolutely refused to go into the house in which the *giraffe* is kept, nor would he visit the elephant, which used formerly to amuse him a great deal. He was afraid of all the large animals, whereas he was very much entertained by the small ones. Among the birds, he was also afraid of the pelican this time—which had never happened before—evidently because of its size again.

"I therefore said to him: 'Do you know why you're afraid of big animals? Big animals have big widdlers, and you're really afraid of big widdlers.'

Hans: "But I've never seen the big animals' widdlers yet."[10]

I: "But you *have* seen a horse's, and a horse is a big animal."

Hans: "Oh, a horse's often. Once at Gmunden when the cart was standing at the door, and once in front of the Head Customs House."

I: "When you were small, you most likely went into a stable at Gmunden . . ."

Hans (interrupting): "Yes, I went into the stable every day at Gmunden when the horses had come home."

I: ". . . and you were most likely frightened when you saw the horse's big widdler one time. But there's no need for you to be frightened of it. Big animals have big widdlers, and little animals have little widdlers."

Hans: "And every one has a widdler. And my widdler will get bigger as I get bigger, because it does grow on to me."

"Here the talk came to an end. During the next few

[10] This was untrue. See his exclamation in front of the lions' cage on pp. 50-51. It was probably the beginning of amnesia resulting from repression.

days it seemed as though his fears had again somewhat increased. He hardly ventured out of the front door, to which he was taken after luncheon."

Hans's last words of comfort throw a light upon the situation and allow us to make some small corrections in his father's assertions. It is true that he was afraid of big animals because he was obliged to think of their big widdlers; but it cannot really be said that he was afraid of big widdlers themselves. Formerly the idea of them had been decidedly pleasurable to him, and he used to make every effort to get a glimpse of one. Since that time this enjoyment had been spoiled for him, owing to the general reversal of pleasure into pain which had come over the whole of his sexual inquiries—in a way which has not yet been explained—and also owing to something which is clearer to us, namely, to certain experiences and reflections which had led to painful conclusions We may conclude from his self-consolatory words ("my widdler will get bigger as I get bigger") that during his observations he had constantly been making comparisons, and that he had remained extremely dissatisfied with the size of his own widdler. Big animals reminded him of this defect, and were for that reason disagreeable to him. But since the whole train of thought was probably incapable of becoming clearly conscious, this painful feeling, too, was turned into morbid anxiety, so that his present anxiety was erected both upon his former pleasure and his present pain. When once a state of anxiety establishes itself, the anxiety swallows up all other feelings; with the progress of repression, and the more those ideas which are charged with affect and which have been conscious move down into the unconscious, all affects are capable of being changed into anxiety.

Hans's singular remark, "because it does grow on to me," makes it possible to guess many things in connection with his consolatory speech which he could not express in words and did not express during the course of the analysis. I shall bridge the gap for a little distance by means of my experiences in the analyses of grown-up people; but I hope the interpolation will not be considered arbitrary or capricious. "It does grow on to me": if the motives of the thought were solace and defiance, we are reminded of his mother's old threat that she should have his widdler cut off if he went on playing with it. At the time it was made, when he was three and a half, this threat had no effect. He calmly replied that then he should widdle with his bottom. It would be the most completely typical procedure if the threat of castration were to have a *deferred* effect, and if he were now, a year and a quarter later, oppressed by the fear of having to lose this precious piece of his ego. In other cases of illness we can observe a similar deferred operation of commands and threats made in childhood, where the interval covers as many decades or more. I even know cases in which a "deferred obedience" on the part of the repression has had a principal share in determining the symptoms of the disease.

The piece of enlightenment which Hans had been given a short time before to the effect that women really do not possess a widdler was bound to have had a shattering effect upon his self-confidence and to have aroused his castration complex. For this reason he resisted the information, and for this reason it had no therapeutic results. Could it be that living beings really did exist which did not possess widdlers? If so, it would no longer be so incredible that they could take his own widdler away, and, as it were, make him into a woman![11]

[11] I cannot so far interrupt the discussion as to demonstrate the typical character of the unconscious train of thought which I think there is here reason for attributing to little Hans. The castration complex is the deepest unconscious root of anti-semitism; for even in the nursery little boys hear that a Jew has something cut off his penis—a piece of his penis, they think—and this gives them a right to despise Jews. And there is no stronger unconscious root for the sense of superiority over women. Weininger (the young philosopher who, highly gifted but sexually deranged, committed suicide after producing his remarkable book, *Geschlecht und Charakter*), in a

"During the night of 27th-28th Hans surprised us by getting out of bed while it was quite dark and coming into our bed. His room is separated from our bedroom by another small room. We asked him why: whether he had been afraid, perhaps. 'No,' he said; 'I'll tell you to-morrow.' He went to sleep in our bed and was then carried back to his own.

"Next day I questioned him closely to discover why he had come in to us during the night; and after some reluctance the following dialogue took place, which I immediately took down in shorthand:

He: "*In the night there was a big giraffe in the room and a crumpled one; and the big one called out because I took the crumpled one away from it. Then it stopped calling out; and then I sat down on the top of the crumpled one.*"

I (puzzled): "What? A crumpled giraffe? How was that?"

He: "Yes." (He quickly fetched a piece of paper, crumpled it up, and said:) "It was crumpled like that."

I: "And you sat down on the top of the crumpled giraffe? How?"

"He again showed me, by sitting down on the ground.

I: "Why did you come into our room?"

He: "I don't know myself."

I: "Were you afraid?"

He: "No. Of course not."

I: "Did you dream about the giraffe?"

He: "No. I didn't dream. I thought it. I thought it all. I'd woken up earlier."

I: "What can it mean: a crumpled giraffe? You know you can't squash a giraffe together like a piece of paper."

---

chapter that has attracted much attention, treated Jews and women with equal hostility and overwhelmed them with the same insults. Being a neurotic, Weininger was completely under the sway of his infantile complexes; and from that standpoint what is common to Jews and women is their relation to the castration complex.

He: "Of course I know. I just thought it. Of course there aren't any really and truly.[12] The crumpled one was all lying on the floor, and I took it away—took hold of it with my hands."

I: "What? Can you take hold of a big giraffe like that with your hands?"

He: "I took hold of the crumpled one with my hand."

I: "Where was the big one in the meantime?"

He: "The big one just stood farther off."

I: "What did you do with the crumpled one?"

He: "I held it in my hand for a bit, till the big one had stopped calling out. And when the big one had stopped calling out, I sat down on top of it."

I: "Why did the big one call out?"

He: "Because I'd taken away the little one from it." (He noticed that I was taking everything down, and asked:) "Why are you writing that down?"

I: "Because I shall send it to a Professor, who can take away your 'nonsense' for you."

He: "Oho! So you've written down as well that Mummy took off her chemise, and you'll give that to the Professor too."

I: "Yes. But he won't understand how you can think that a giraffe can be crumpled up."

He: "Just tell him I don't know myself, and then he won't ask. But if he asks what the crumpled giraffe is, then he can write to us, and we can write back, or let's write at once that I don't know myself."

I: "But why did you come in in the night?"

He: "I don't know."

I: "Just tell me quickly what you're thinking of."

He (jokingly): "Of raspberry syrup."

I: "What else?"

He: "A gun for shooting people dead with."[13]

⎫
⎬ His wishes.
⎭

[12] In his own language Hans was saying quite definitely that it was a phantasy.

[13] At this point his father in his perplexity was trying to practise the classical technique of psychoanalysis. This did

I: "You're sure you didn't dream it?"

He: "Quite sure; no, I'm quite certain of it."

He proceeded: "Mummy begged me so long to tell her why I came in in the night. But I didn't want to say, because I felt ashamed with Mummy at first."

I: "Why?"

He: "I didn't know."

"My wife had in fact examined him all the morning, till he had told her the giraffe story."

That same day his father discovered the solution of the giraffe phantasy.

"The big giraffe is myself, or rather my big penis (the long neck), and the crumpled giraffe is my wife, or rather her genital organ. It is therefore the result of the enlightenment he has had.

"Giraffe: see the expedition to Schönbrunn. Moreover, he has a picture of a giraffe and an elephant hanging over his bed.

"The whole thing is a reproduction of a scene which has been gone through almost every morning for the last few days. Hans always comes in to us in the early morning, and my wife cannot resist taking him into bed with her for a few minutes. Thereupon I always begin to warn her not to take him in bed with her ('the big one called out because I'd taken the crumpled one away from it'); and she answers now and then, rather irritated, no doubt, that it's all nonsense, that one minute is after all of no importance, and so on. Then Hans stays with her a little while. ('Then the big giraffe stopped calling out; and then I sat down on top of the crumpled one.')

"Thus the solution of this matrimonial scene transposed into giraffe life is this: he was seized in the night with a longing for his mother, for her caresses, for her genital

not lead to much; but the result, such as it was, can be given a meaning in the light of later disclosures.

organ, and came into our bedroom for that reason. The whole thing is a continuation of his fear of horses."

I have only this to add to his father's penetrating interpretation. The "*sitting* down on top of" was probably Hans's representation of taking *possession*.[14] But the whole thing was a phantasy of defiance connected with his satisfaction at the triumph over his father's resistance. "Call out as much as you like! but Mummy takes me into bed all the same, and Mummy belongs to me!" It is therefore justifiable, as his father suspected, to divine behind the phantasy a fear that his mother did not like him, because his widdler was not comparable to his father's.

Next morning his father was able to get his interpretation confirmed.

"On Sunday, March 29th, I went with Hans to Lainz. I jokingly took leave of my wife at the door with the words: 'Good-bye, big giraffe!' 'Why giraffe?' asked Hans. 'Mummy's the big giraffe,' I replied; to which Hans rejoined: 'Oh yes! And Hanna's the crumpled giraffe, isn't she?'

"In the train I explained the giraffe phantasy to him, upon which he said: 'Yes, that's right.' And when I said to him that I was the big giraffe, and that its long neck had reminded him of a widdler, he said: 'Mummy has a neck like a giraffe, too. I saw, when she was washing her white neck.'[15]

"On Monday, March 30th, in the morning, Hans came to me and said: 'I say! I thought two things this morning!'

---

[14] [The German word for "possession" ("*Besitz*") shows its etymological connection with the phrase used by little Hans ("*sich draufsetzen*") more obviously than the English.—*Trans.*]

[15] Hans only confirmed the interpretation of the two giraffes as his father and mother, and not the sexual symbolism, according to which the giraffe itself represented the penis. This symbolism was probably correct, but we really cannot ask more of Hans.

'What was the first?' 'I was with you at Schönbrunn where the sheep are; and then we crawled through under the ropes, and then we told the policeman at the end of the garden, and he grabbed hold of us.' He had forgotten the second thing.

"I add the following remark upon this. When we wanted to visit the sheep on Sunday, we found that a space in the gardens was shut off by a rope, so that we were unable to get to them. Hans was very much astonished that the space should be shut off only with a rope, which it would be quite easy to slip under. I told him that respectable people didn't crawl under the rope. He said it would be quite easy; whereupon I replied that a policeman might come along and take one off. There is a life-guardsman on duty at the entrance of Schönbrunn; and I once told Hans that he arrested naughty children.

"After we returned from our visit to you, which took place the same day, Hans confessed to yet another little bit of craving to do something forbidden: 'I say, I thought something this morning again.' 'What?' 'I went with you in the train, and we smashed a window, and the policeman took us off with him.' "

A most suitable continuation of the giraffe phantasy. He had a suspicion that to take possession of his mother was forbidden; he had come up against the incest-barrier. But he regarded it as forbidden in itself. His father was with him each time in the forbidden exploits which he carried out in his imagination, and was locked up with him. His father, he thought, also did that enigmatic forbidden something with his mother which he replaced by an act of violence such as smashing a window-pane or forcing a way into an enclosed space.

That afternoon the father and son visited me during my consulting hours. I already knew the queer little chap, and with all his self-assurance he was yet so amiable that I had always been glad to see him. I do not know whether he remembered me, but he behaved irreproachably and like a perfectly reasonable member of human society. The consultation was a short one. His father opened it by remarking that, in spite of all the pieces of enlightenment we had given Hans, his fear of horses had not yet diminished. We were also forced to confess that the connections between the horses he was afraid of and the affectionate feelings towards his mother which had been revealed were by no means abundant. Certain details which I now learnt—to the effect that he was particularly bothered by what horses wear in front of their eyes and by the black round their mouths—were certainly not to be explained from what we knew. But as I saw the two of them sitting in front of me and at the same time heard Hans's description of his anxiety-horses, a further piece of the solution shot through my mind, and a piece which I could well understand might escape his father. I asked Hans jokingly whether his horses wore eyeglasses, to which he replied that they did not. I then asked him whether his father wore eyeglasses, to which, against all the evidence, he once more said no. Finally I asked him whether by "the black round the mouth" he meant a moustache; and I then disclosed to him that he was afraid of his father, precisely because he was so fond of his mother. It must be, I told him, that he thought his father was angry with him on that account; but this was not so, his father was fond of him in spite of it, and he might admit everything to him without any fear. Long before he was in the world, I went on, I had known that a little Hans would come who would be so fond of his mother that he would be bound to feel afraid of his father because of it; and I had told his father this. "But why do you think I'm angry with you?" his father interrupted me at this point; "have I ever scolded you or hit you?" Hans corrected him: "Oh yes! You have hit me." "That's not true. When was it, anyhow?" "This morning," answered the little boy; and his father recollected that Hans had quite unexpectedly butted his head into his stomach, so that he had given him as it were a reflex blow with his hand. It was remarkable that he had not brought this detail into connection with the neurosis; but he now recognized it as an expression of the little boy's hostile disposition towards him, and perhaps also as a manifestation of a need for getting punished for it.[16]

"Does the Professor talk to God," Hans asked his father on the way home, "as he can tell all that beforehand?" I should be extraordinarily proud of this recognition out of the mouth of a child, if I had not myself provoked it by my joking boastfulness. From the date of this consultation I received almost daily reports of the alterations in the little patient's condition. It was not to be expected that he should be freed from his anxiety at a single blow by the information I gave him; but it became apparent that a possibility had now been offered him of bringing forward his unconscious productions and of unfolding his phobia. From that time forward he carried out a programme which I was able to announce to his father in advance.

"April 2nd. The *first real improvement* is to be noted. While formerly he could never be induced to go out of the street-door for very long, and always ran back into the house with every sign of fright if horses came along, this time he stayed in front of the street-door for an hour— even while carts were driving past, which happens fairly often in our street. Every now and then he ran into the house when he saw a cart approaching in the distance, but he turned round at once as though he were changing his mind. In any case there is only a trace of the anxiety left, and the progress since his enlightenment is unmistakable.

"In the evening he said: 'We get as far as the street-door now, so we'll go into the Stadtpark too.'

"On April 3rd, in the morning he came into bed with me, whereas for the last few days he had not been coming any more and had even seemed to be proud of not doing so. 'And why have you come to-day?' I asked.

Hans: "When I'm not frightened I shan't come any more."

[16] Later on the boy repeated his reaction towards his father in a clearer and more complete manner, by first hitting his father on the hand and then affectionately kissing the same hand.

I: "So you come in to me because you're frightened?"

Hans: "When I'm not with you I'm frightened; when I'm not in bed with you, then I'm frightened. When I'm not frightened any more I shan't come any more."

I: "So you're fond of me and you feel anxious when you're in your bed in the morning? and that's why you come in to me?"

Hans: "Yes. Why did you tell me I'm fond of *Mummy* and that's why I'm frightened, when I'm fond of *you?*"

Here the little boy was displaying a really unusual degree of clarity. He was bringing to notice the fact that his love for his father was wrestling with his hostility towards him in his capacity of rival with his mother; and he was reproaching his father with not having yet drawn his attention to this interplay of forces, which was bound to end in anxiety. His father did not entirely understand him as yet, for during this conversation he only succeeded in convincing himself of the little boy's hostility towards him, the existence of which I had asserted during our consultation. The following dialogue, which I nevertheless give without alteration, is really of more importance in connection with the progress of the father's enlightenment than with the little patient.

"Unfortunately I did not immediately grasp the meaning of this reproach. Because Hans is fond of his mother he evidently wants to get me out of the way, and he would then be in his father's place. This suppressed hostile wish is turned into anxiety *about* his father, and he comes in to me in the morning to see if I have gone away. Unfortunately at the moment I did not understand this, and said to him:

"When you're alone, you're just anxious for me and come in to me."

Hans: "When you're away, I'm afraid you're not coming home."

I: "And have I ever threatened you that I shan't come home?"

Hans: "Not you, but Mummy. Mummy's told me she

won't come back." (He had probably been naughty, and she had threatened to go away.)

I: "She said that because you were naughty."

Hans: "Yes."

I: "So you're afraid I'm going away because you were naughty; that's why you come in to me."

"When I got up from table after breakfast Hans said: 'Daddy, don't trot away from me!' I was struck by his saying 'trot' instead of 'run,' and replied: 'Oho! So you're afraid of the horse trotting away from you.' Upon which he laughed."

We know that this part of Hans's morbid anxiety had two constituents: there was fear *of* his father and fear *for* his father. The former was derived from his hostility towards his father, and the latter from the conflict between his affection, which was exaggerated at this point by way of compensation, and his hostility.

His father proceeds: "This is no doubt the beginning of an important phase. His motive for at the most just venturing outside the house but not going away from it, and for turning round at the first attack of anxiety when he is half-way, is his fear of not finding his parents at home because they have gone away. He sticks to the house from love of his mother, and he is afraid of my going away because of the hostile wishes that he nourishes against me—for then *he* would be the father.

"In the summer I used to be constantly leaving Gmunden for Vienna on business, and he was then the father. You will remember that his fear of horses is connected with the episode at Gmunden when a horse was to take Lizzi's luggage to the station. The repressed wish that I should drive to the station, for then he would be alone with his mother (the wish that 'the horse should drive off'), is turned into fear of the horse's driving off; and in fact nothing throws him into greater alarm than when a cart drives off from the courtyard of the Head Customs House (which is just opposite our flat) and the horses start moving.

"This new phase (hostile sentiments towards his father) could only come out after he knew that I was not angry because he was so fond of his mother.

"In the afternoon I went out in front of the street-door with him again; he again went out in front of the house, and stayed there even when carts went past. In the case of only a few carts he was afraid, and ran into the entrance-hall. He also said to me in explanation: 'Not all white horses bite.' That is to say: owing to the analysis some white horses have already been recognized as 'Daddy,' and they no longer bite; but there are others still left over which do bite.

"The position of our street-door is as follows: Opposite it is the warehouse of the Office for the Taxation of Food-Stuffs, with a loading dock at which carts are driving up all day long to fetch away boxes, packing-cases, etc. This courtyard is cut off from the street by railings; and the entrance gates to the courtyard are opposite our house (Fig. 2). I have noticed for some days that Hans is

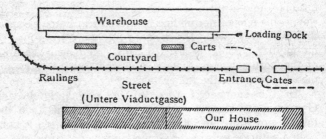

Fig. 2

specially frightened when carts drive into or out of the yard, a process which involves their taking a corner. I asked at the time why he was so much afraid, and he replied: '*I'm afraid the horses will fall down when the cart turns* (A).' He is equally frightened when carts standing at the loading dock start moving in order to drive off (B). Further (C), he is more frightened of large dray-horses than of small horses, and of rough farm-horses than of smart horses (such as those in a carriage and pair). He is also more frightened when a vehicle drives past quickly (D) than when the horses trot up slowly. These differentiations have, of course, only come to light clearly during the last few days."

I should be inclined to say that, in consequence of the analysis, not only the patient but his phobia too had plucked up courage and was venturing to show itself.

"On April 5th Hans came in to our bedroom again, and was sent back to his own bed. I said to him: 'As long as you come into our room in the mornings, your fear of horses won't get better.' He was defiant, however, and replied: 'I shall come in all the same, even if I *am* afraid.' So he will not let himself be forbidden to visit his mother.

"After breakfast we were to go downstairs. Hans was delighted, and planned that, instead of stopping in front of the street-door as usual, he should go across the street into the yard, where he had often enough seen street-boys playing. I told him I should be pleased if he were to go across, and took the opportunity of asking him why he is so much afraid when the loaded carts at the loading dock start moving (B).

Hans: "I'm afraid of standing by the cart and the cart driving off quick, and of my standing on it and wanting to get on to the board (the loading dock), and my driving off in the cart."

I: "And if the cart stands still? Aren't you afraid then? Why not?"

Hans: "If the cart stands still, then I can get on to the cart quick and get on to the board."

"(Hans was planning, therefore, to climb over a cart on to the loading dock, and is afraid of the cart driving away while he is on it.)

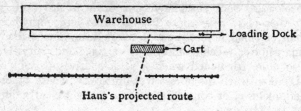

Fig. 3

I: "Perhaps you're afraid you won't come home any more if you drive away in the cart?"

Hans: "Oh no! I can always come back to Mamma, in the cart or in a cab. I can tell him the number of the house too."

I: "Then why *are* you afraid?"

Hans: "I don't know. But the Professor'll know. D'you think he'll know?"

I: "And why do you want to get over on to the board?"

Hans: "Because I've never been up there, and I should so much like to be there; and d'you know why I should like to go there? Because I should like to load and unload the packages, and I should like to climb about on the packages there. I should so like to climb about there. D'you know who I learnt the climbing about from? Some boys climbed on the packages, and I saw them, and I want to do it too."

"His wish was not fulfilled. For when Hans ventured once more in front of the street-door, the few steps across the street and into the courtyard awoke too great resistances in him, because carts were constantly driving into the yard."

The Professor only knows that the game which Hans intended to play with the loaded carts must have stood in the relation of a symbolic substitute to some other wish as to which he had so far uttered no word. But, if it did not seem too daring, this wish might already, even at this stage, be constructed.

"In the afternoon we again went out in front of the street-door, and when I returned I asked Hans:

"Which horses are you actually most afraid of?"

Hans: "All of them."

I: "That's not true."

Hans: "I'm most afraid of horses with a thing on their mouths."

I: "What do you mean? The piece of iron they have in their mouths?"

Hans: "No. They have something black on their mouths." (He covered his mouth with his hand.)

I: "What? A moustache, perhaps?"

Hans (laughing): "Oh no!"

I: "Have they all got it?"

Hans: "No, only a few of them."

I: "What is it that they've got on their mouths?"

Hans: "A black thing." (I think in reality it must be the thick piece of harness that dray-horses wear over their noses.)

"And I'm most afraid of furniture-vans, too."

I: "Why?"

Hans: "I think when furniture-horses are dragging a heavy van they'll fall down."

I: "So you're not afraid with a small cart?"

Hans: "No. I'm not afraid with a small cart or with a post-office van. I'm most afraid too when a bus comes along."

Fig. 4

I: "Why? Because it's so big?"

Hans: "No. Because once a horse in a bus fell down."

I: "When?"

Hans: "Once when I went out with Mummy in spite of my 'nonsense,' when I bought the waistcoat." (This was subsequently confirmed by his mother.)

I: "What did you think when the horse fell down?"

Hans: "Now it'll always be like this. All horses in buses'll fall down."

I: "In all buses?"

Hans: "Yes. And in furniture-vans too. Not often in furniture-vans."

I: "You had your nonsense already at that time?"

Hans: "No. I only got it then. When the horse in the bus fell down, it gave me such a fright, really! That was when I got the nonsense."

I: "But the nonsense was that you thought a horse would bite you. And now you say you were afraid a horse would fall down."

Hans: "Fall down and bite."[17]

I: "Why did it give you such a fright?"

Hans: "Because the horse went like this with its feet." (He lay down on the ground and showed me how it kicked about.) "It gave me a fright *because it made a row with its feet.*"

I: "Where did you go with Mummy that day?"

Hans: "First to the Skating Rink, then to a *café*, then to buy a waistcoat, then to the pastry-cook's with Mummy, and then home in the evening; we went back through the Stadtpark." (All of this was confirmed by my wife, as well as the fact that the anxiety broke out immediately after-wards.)

I: "Was the horse dead when it fell down?"

Hans: "Yes!"

I: "How do you know that?"

---

[17] Hans was right, however improbable this collocation may sound. The train of thought, as we shall see, was that the horse (his father) would bite him because of his wish that it (his father) should fall down.

Hans: "Because I saw it." (He laughed.) "No, it wasn't a bit dead."

I: "Perhaps you thought it was dead?"

Hans: "No. Certainly not. I only said it as a joke." (His expression at the moment, however, had been serious.)

"As he was tired, I let him run off. He only told me besides this that he had first been afraid of bus-horses, then of all others, and only in the end of furniture-van horses.

"On the way back from Lainz there were a few more questions:

I: "When the bus-horse fell down, what colour was it? White, red, brown, grey?"

Hans: "Black. Both horses were black."

I: "Was it big or little?"

Hans: "Big."

I: "Fat or thin?"

Hans: "Fat. Very big and fat."

I: "When the horse fell down, did you think of your daddy?"

Hans: "Perhaps. Yes. It's possible."

His father's investigations may have been without success at many points; but it does no harm to make acquaintance at close quarters with a phobia of this sort—which one is apt to name after its new objects. In this way we get to see how diffuse it really is. It goes on to horses and on to carts, on to the fact that horses fall down and that they bite, on to horses of a particular character, on to carts that are heavily loaded. We may at once explain that all of these characteristics are derived from the circumstance that the anxiety had originally no reference at all to horses but was transposed on to them secondarily and had now become fixed upon those elements of the horse-complex which showed themselves well adapted for certain transferences. We must specially acknowledge one most important result of the boy's examination by his father. We have learned the immediate exciting cause after which the

phobia broke out. This was when the boy saw a big heavy
horse fall down; and one at least of the interpretations of
this impression seems to be that emphasized by his father,
namely, that Hans at that moment perceived a wish that
his father might in the same way fall down—and be dead.
His serious expression as he was telling the story no doubt
referred to this unconscious meaning. May there not have
been yet another meaning concealed behind all this? And
what can have been the significance of the making a row
with its legs?

"For some time Hans has been playing horses in the
room; he trots about, falls down, kicks about with his feet,
and neighs. Once he tied a small bag on like a nose-bag.
He has repeatedly run up to me and bitten me."

In this way he was accepting the last interpretations
more decidedly than he could in words, but naturally with
a change of parts, for the game was in the service of a
wish-phantasy. Thus he was the horse, he bit his father,
and in this way he was identifying himself with his father.

"I have noticed for the last two days that Hans has been
defying me in the most decided manner, not impudently,
but in the highest spirits. Is it because he is no longer
afraid of me—the horse?

"April 6th. Went out with Hans in front of the house in
the afternoon. At every horse that passed I asked him if
he saw the 'black on its mouth'; he said 'no' every time. I
asked him what the black really looked like; he said it was
black iron. My first idea, that he meant the thick leather
straps that are part of the harness of dray-horses, is therefore unconfirmed. I asked him if the 'black' reminded him
of a moustache, and he said: 'Only by its colour.' So I do
not yet know what it really is.

"The fear has diminished; this time he ventured as far
as the next-door house, but turned round quickly when he
heard the sound of horses' hoofs in the distance. When a
cart drew up at our door and came to a stop, he became
frightened and ran into the house, because the horse began
pawing with its foot. I asked him why he was afraid, and

whether perhaps he was nervous because the horse had done like this (and I stamped with my foot). He said: 'Don't make such a row with your feet!' Compare his remark upon the fallen bus-horse.

"He was particularly terrified by a furniture-van passing by. At that he ran right inside the house. 'Doesn't a furniture-van like that,' I asked him unconcernedly, 'really look like a bus?' He said nothing. I repeated the question, and he then said: 'Why, of course! Otherwise I shouldn't be so afraid of a furniture-van.'

"April 7th. I asked again to-day what the 'black on the horses' mouths' looked like. Hans said: 'Like a muzzle.' The curious thing is that for the last three days not a single horse has passed on which he could point out this 'muzzle.' I myself have seen no such horse on any of my walks, although Hans asseverates that such horses do exist. I suspect that some sort of horses' bridle—the thick piece of harness round their mouths, perhaps—really reminded him of a moustache, and that after I alluded to this this fear disappeared as well.

"Hans's improvement is constant. The radius of his circle of activity with the street-door as its centre is ever wider. He has even accomplished the feat, which has hitherto been impossible for him, of running across to the pavement opposite. All the fear that remains is connected with the bus scene, the meaning of which is not yet clear to me.

"April 9th. This morning Hans came in to me while I was washing and bare to the waist.

Hans: "Daddy, you *are* lovely! You're so white."

I: "Yes. Like a white horse."

Hans: "The only black thing's your moustache." (Continuing) "Or perhaps it's a black muzzle?"

"I told him then that I had been to see the Professor the evening before, and said: 'There's one thing he wants to know.' 'I *am* curious,' remarked Hans.

"I told him I knew on what occasions it was that he made a row with his feet. 'Oh, yes!' he interrupted me, 'when I'm cross, or when I have to do "lumf" and would rather play.' (He has a habit, it is true, of making a row with his feet, *i.e.* of stamping, when he is angry.—'Doing lumf' means doing number two. When Hans was small he said one day when he got off the chamber: 'Look at the lumf [German: *"lumpf"*].' He meant 'stocking' [German: *'strumpf'*], with reference to its shape and colour. This designation has been preserved to this day.—In very early days, when he had to be put on the chamber, and refused to leave off playing, he used to stamp his feet in a rage, and kick about, and sometimes throw himself on the ground.)

" 'And you kick about with your feet as well, when you have to widdle and don't want to go, because you'd rather go on playing.'

He: "Oh, I must widdle." And he went out of the room—by way of confirmation, no doubt."

In the course of his visit his father had asked me what Hans could have been reminded of by the fallen horse kicking about with its feet. I had suggested that that may have been his own reaction when he retained his urine. Hans now confirmed this by means of the re-emergence during the conversation of a desire to urinate; and he added some other significations of the making a row with the feet.

"We then went out in front of the street-door. When a coal-cart came along, he said to me: 'Daddy, I'm very much afraid of coal-carts, too.'

I: "Perhaps that's because they're as big as buses, too."
Hans: "Yes; and because they're so heavily loaded, and the horses have so much to drag and might easily fall down. If a cart's empty, I'm not afraid." It is a fact, as I have already remarked, that only heavy vehicles throw him into a state of anxiety."

Nevertheless, the situation was decidedly obscure. The analysis was making little progress; and I am afraid the reader will soon begin to find this description of it tedious. Every analysis, however, has dark periods of this kind. But Hans was now on the point of leading us into an unexpected region.

"I came home and was speaking to my wife, who had made various purchases which she was showing me. Among them was a pair of yellow ladies' drawers. Hans exclaimed 'Ugh!' two or three times, threw himself on the ground, and spat. My wife said he had done this two or three times already when he had seen the drawers.

"Why do you say 'Ugh'?" I asked.

Hans: "Because of the drawers."

I: "Why? Because of their colour? Because they're yellow, and remind you of lumf or widdle?"

Hans: "Lumf isn't yellow. It's white or black."—Immediately afterwards: "I say, is it easy to do lumf if you eat cheese?" (I had once told him so, when he asked me why I ate cheese.)

I: "Yes."

Hans: "That's why you go straight off every morning and do lumf? I should so much like to eat cheese with my bread-and-butter."

"He had already asked me yesterday as he was jumping about in the street: 'I say, it's true, isn't it, if you jump about a lot you can do lumf easily?'—There has been trouble with his stools from the very first; and aperients and enemas have frequently been necessary. At one time his habitual constipation was so great that my wife called in Dr. L. He was of opinion that Hans was overfed, which was in fact the case, and recommended a more moderate diet—and the condition was at once brought to an end. Recently the constipation has again made its appearance more frequently.

"After luncheon I said to him: 'We'll write to the Professor again,' and he dictated to me: 'When I saw the yellow drawers I said "Ugh! that makes me spit!" and threw myself down and shut my eyes and didn't look.'

I: "Why?"

Hans: "Because I saw the yellow drawers; and I did the same sort of thing with the black drawers too.[18] The black ones are the same sort of drawers, only they were black." (Interrupting himself) "I say, I *am* glad. I'm always so glad when I can write to the Professor."

I: "Why did you say 'Ugh'? Were you disgusted?"

Hans: "Yes, because I saw that. I thought I should have to do lumf."

I: "Why?"

Hans: "I don't know."

I: "When did you see the black drawers?"

Hans: "Once, when Anna (our maid) had been here a long time—with Mamma—she brought them home just after she'd bought them." (This statement was confirmed by my wife.)

I: "Were you disgusted then, too?"

Hans: "Yes."

I: "Have you seen Mummy in drawers like that?"

Hans: "No."

I: "When she was dressing?"

Hans: "When she bought the yellow ones I'd seen them once before already." (This is contradicted. He saw the yellow ones for the first time when his mother bought them.) "She's got the black ones on to-day too" (correct), "because I saw her take them off in the morning."

I: "What? She took off the black drawers in the morning?"

Hans: "In the morning when she went out she took off the black drawers, and when she came back she put the black ones on again."

"I asked my wife about this, as it seemed to me absurd. She said it was entirely untrue. Of course she had not changed her drawers when she went out.

"I at once asked Hans about it: 'You told me that Mummy had put on some black drawers, and that when

[18] "For the last few weeks my wife has possessed a pair of black bloomers for wearing on cycling tours."

she went out she took them off, and that when she came back she put them on again. But Mummy says it's not true.'

Hans: "I think perhaps I may have forgotten she didn't take them off." (Impatiently) "Oh, do let me alone."

I have a few comments to make at this point on the business of the drawers. It was obviously mere hypocrisy on Hans's part to pretend to be so glad of the opportunity of giving an account of the affair. In the end he threw the mask aside and was rude to his father. It was a question of things which had once afforded him *a great deal of pleasure,* but of which, now that repression had set in, he was very much ashamed, and at which he professed to be disgusted. He told some downright lies so as to disguise the circumstances in which he had seen his mother change her drawers. In reality, the putting on and taking off of her drawers belonged to the "lumf" context. His father was perfectly aware of what it was all about and of what Hans was trying to conceal.

"I asked my wife whether Hans was often with her when she went to the W.C. 'Yes,' she said, 'often. He goes on pestering me till I let him. Children are all like that.' "

Nevertheless, it is worth bearing carefully in mind the desire, which Hans had already repressed, for seeing his mother doing lumf.

"We went out in front of the house. He was in very good spirits and was prancing about all the time like a horse. So I said: 'Now, who is it that's the bus-horse? Me, you, or Mummy?'

Hans (promptly): "I am; I'm a young horse."

"During the period when his anxiety was at its height, and he was frightened at seeing horses frisking, he asked me why they did it; and to reassure him I said: 'Those are young horses, you see, and they frisk about like little boys. You frisk about too, and you're a little boy.' Since then, whenever he has seen horses frisking, he has said: 'That's right; those are young horses!'

"As we were going upstairs I asked him almost without thinking: 'Used you to play at horses with the children at Gmunden?'

He: "Yes." (Thoughtfully) "I think that was how I got the nonsense."

I: "Who was the horse?"

He: "I was; and Berta was the coachman."

I: "Did you fall down by any chance, when you were a horse?"

Hans: "No. When Berta said 'Gee-up,' I ran ever so quick; I just raced along."[19]

I: "You never played at buses?"

Hans: "No. At ordinary carts, and horses without carts. When a horse has a cart, it can go without a cart just as well, and the cart can stay at home."

I: "Used you often to play at horses?"

Hans: "Very often. Fritzl[20] was the horse once, too, and Franzl the coachman; and Fritzl ran ever so fast and all at once he hit his foot on a stone and bled."

I: "Perhaps he fell down?"

Hans: "No. He put his foot in some water and then wrapped it up."[21]

I: "Were you often the horse?"

Hans: "Oh, yes."

I: "And that was how you got the nonsense?"

Hans: "Because they kept on saying ' 'cos of the horse,' ' 'cos of the horse' " (he put a stress on the " 'cos"); "so perhaps I got the nonsense because they talked like that; ' 'cos of the horse.' "[22]

---

[19] "Hans had a set of toy harness with bells."

[20] Another of the landlord's children, as we are already aware.

[21] See below. His father was quite right in suspecting that Fritzl fell down.

[22] I may explain that Hans was not maintaining that he had got the nonsense *at that time* but *in that connection.* Indeed, it must have been so, for theoretical considerations require that what is to-day the object of a phobia must at one time in the

For a while Hans's father pursued his inquiry fruitlessly along other paths.

I: "Did they tell you anything about horses?"
Hans: "Yes."
I: "What?"
Hans: "I've forgotten."
I: "Perhaps they told you about their widdlers?"
Hans: "Oh, no."
I: "Were you frightened of horses already then?"
Hans: "Oh, no. I wasn't frightened at all."
I: "Perhaps Berta told you that horses——"
Hans (interrupting): "——widdle? No."

"On April 10th I took up our conversation of the day before, and tried to discover what his ' 'cos of the horse' meant. Hans could not remember; he only knew that some children had stood outside the front door one morning and had said, ' 'cos of the horse, 'cos of the horse!' He had been there himself. When I pressed him more closely, he declared that they had not said ' 'cos of the horse' at all, but that he had remembered wrong.

I: "But you and the others were often in the stables. You must surely have talked about horses there."—"We didn't."—"What did you talk about?"—"Nothing."— "Such a lot of children, and nothing to talk about?"—"We did talk about something, but not about horses."—"Well, what was it?"—"I don't remember any more."

---

past have been the source of a high degree of pleasure. I may at the same time complete what the child was unable to express, and add that the little word *"wegen"* ["because of," " 'cos of"] was the means of enabling the phobia to extend from horses on to *"Wagen"* ["vehicles"] or, as Hans was accustomed to pronounce the word and hear it pronounced, *"Wägen"* [pronounced exactly like *"wegen"*]. It must never be forgotten how much more concretely children treat words than grown-up people do, and consequently how much more significant for them are similarities of sound in words.

"I allowed the matter to drop, as the resistances were evidently too great,[23] and went on to the following question: 'Did you like playing with Berta?'

He: "Yes, very much; but not with Olga. D'you know what Olga did? I was given a paper ball once by Grete up there at Gmunden, and Olga tore it all to pieces. Berta would never have torn my ball. I liked playing with Berta very much."

I: "Did you see what Berta's widdler looked like?"

He: "No, but I saw the horses'; because I was always in the stables, and so I saw the horses' widdlers."

I: "And so you were curious and wanted to know what Berta's and Mummy's widdlers looked like?"

He: "Yes."

"I reminded him of how he had once complained to me that the little girls always wanted to look on while he was widdling.

He: "Berta always looked on at me too" (he spoke with great satisfaction and not at all resentfully); "often she did. I used to widdle in the little garden where the radishes were, and she stood outside the front door and looked on at me."

I: "And when she widdled, did you look on?"

He: "She used to go to the W.C."

I: "And you were curious?"

He: "I was inside the W.C. when she was in it."

(This was a fact. The servants told us about it once, and I recollect that we forbade Hans to do it.)

I: "Did you tell her you wanted to go in?"

He: "I went in alone and because Berta let me. There's nothing shameful in that."

[23] In point of fact there was nothing more to be got out of it than Hans's verbal association, and this had escaped his father. Here is a good instance of conditions under which an analyst's efforts are wasted.

I: "And you'd have liked to see her widdler?"

He: "Yes, but I didn't see it."

"I then reminded him of the dream about playing forfeits that he had had at Gmunden, and said: 'When you were at Gmunden did you want Berta to make you widdle?'

He: "I never said so to her."

I: "Why didn't you ever say so to her?"

He: "Because I didn't think of it." (Interrupting himself) "If I write everything to the Professor, my nonsense'll soon be over, won't it?"

I: "Why did you want Berta to make you widdle?"

He: "I don't know. Because she looked on at me."

I: "Did you think to yourself she should put her hand to your widdler?"

He: "Yes." (Changing the subject) "It was such fun at Gmunden. In the little garden where the radishes were there was a little sand-heap, and I used to play there with my spade."

(This was the garden where he used always to widdle.)

I: "Did you put your hand to your widdler at Gmunden, when you were in bed?"

He: "No. Not then; I slept so well at Gmunden that I never thought of it at all. The only times I did it was at——Street[24] and now."

I: "But Berta never put her hand to your widdler?"

He: "She never did, no; because I never told her to."

I: "Well, and when was it you wanted her to?"

He: "Oh, at Gmunden once."

I: "Only once?"

He: "Well, now and then."

I: "She used always to look on at you when you widdled; perhaps she was curious to know how you did it?"

He: "Perhaps she was curious to know what my widdler looked like."

[24] The flat they were in before the move.

I: "But you were curious too. Only about Berta?"

He: "About Berta, and about Olga."

I: "About who else?"

He: "About no one else."

I: "You know that's not true. About Mummy too."

He: "Oh, yes, about Mummy."

I: "But now you're not curious any more. You know what Hanna's widdler looks like, don't you?"

He: "It'll grow, though, won't it?"[25]

I: "Yes, of course. But when it's grown it won't look like yours."

He: "I know that. It'll be the same" (*sc.* as it now is) "only bigger."

I: "When we were at Gmunden, were you curious when your Mamma undressed?"

He: "Yes. And then when Hanna was in her bath I saw her widdler."

I: "And Mummy's too?"

He: "No."

I: "You were disgusted when you saw Mummy's drawers?"

He: "Only when I saw the black ones—when she bought them—then I spat. But I don't spit when she puts her drawers on or takes them off. *I spit because the black drawers are black like a lumf and the yellow ones like widdle, and then I think I've got to widdle.* When Mummy has her drawers on I don't see them; she's got her clothes on over them."

I: "And when she takes off her clothes?"

He: "I don't spit then either. But when her drawers are new they look like a lumf. When they're old, the colour goes away and they get dirty. When you buy them they're quite clean, but at home they've been made dirty. When they're bought they're new, and when they're not bought they're old."

I: "Then you aren't disgusted by old ones?"

[25] Hans wishes to be assured that his own widdler will grow.

He: "When they're old they're much blacker than a lumf, aren't they? They're just a bit blacker."[26]

I: "Have you often been into the W.C. with Mummy?"

He: "Very often."

I: "And were you disgusted?"

He: "Yes. . . . No."

I: "You like being there when Mummy widdles or does lumf?"

He: "Yes, very much."

I: "Why do you like it so much?"

He: "I don't know."

I: "Because you think you'll see her widdler."

He: "Yes, I do think that."

I: "But why won't you ever go into the W.C. at Lainz?"

"(At Lainz he always begs me not to take him into the W.C.; he was frightened once by the noise of the flush.)

He: "Perhaps it's because it makes a row when you pull the plug."

I: "And then you're afraid."

He: "Yes."

I: "And what about our W.C. here?"

He: "Here I'm not. At Lainz it gives me a fright when you pull the plug. And when I'm inside and the water rushes down, then it gives me a fright too."

"And, 'just to show me that he wasn't frightened in our flat,' he made me go into the W.C. and set the flush in motion. He then explained to me:

" 'First there's a loud row, and then a loose one.' (This is when the water comes down.) 'When there's a loud row

---

[26] Our young man was here wrestling with a subject of which he was not equal to giving a clear exposition; so that there is some difficulty in understanding him. He may perhaps have meant that the drawers only recalled his feelings of disgust when he saw them on their own account; as soon as his mother had them on, he ceased to connect them with lumf or widdle, and they then interested him in a different way.

I'd rather stay inside, and when there's a soft one I'd rather go out.'

I: "Because you're afraid?"

He: "Because if there's a loud row I always so much like to see it"—(correcting himself) "to hear it; so I'd rather stay inside and hear it properly."

I: "What does a loud row remind you of?"

He: "That I've got to do lumf in the W.C." (The same thing, that is, that the black drawers reminded him of.)

I: "Why?"

He: "I don't know. A loud row sounds as though you were doing lumf. A big row reminds me of lumf, and a little one of widdle." (Cf. the black and the yellow drawers.)

I: "I say, wasn't the bus-horse the same colour as a lumf?" (According to his account it had been black.)

He (very much struck): "Yes."

At this point I must put in a few words. Hans's father was asking too many questions, and was pressing the inquiry along his own lines instead of allowing the little boy to express his thoughts. For this reason the analysis began to be obscure and uncertain. Hans went his own way and would produce nothing if attempts were made to draw him off it. For the moment his interest was evidently centred upon lumf and widdle, but we cannot tell why. Just as little satisfactory light was thrown upon the business of the row as upon that of the yellow and black drawers. I suspect that the boy's sharp ears had clearly detected the difference between the sounds made by a man urinating and a woman. The analysis succeeded in forcing the material somewhat artificially into an expression of the distinction between the two different calls of nature. I can only advise those of my readers who have not as yet themselves conducted an analysis not to try to understand everything at once, but to give a kind of unbiassed attention to every point that arises and to await further developments.

"April 11th. This morning Hans came into our room again and was sent away, as he always has been for the last few days.

"Later on, he began: 'Daddy, I thought something: *I was in the bath,*[27] *and then the plumber came and unscrewed it.*[28] *Then he took a big borer and stuck it into my stomach.*' "

Hans's father translated this phantasy as follows: " 'I was in bed with Mamma. Then Papa came and drove me away. With his big penis he pushed me out of my place by Mamma.' "

Let us suspend our judgement for the present.

"He went on to relate a second idea that he had had: 'We were travelling in the train to Gmunden. In the station we put on our clothes; but we couldn't get it done in time, and the train carried us on.'

"Later on, I asked: 'Have you ever seen a horse doing lumf?'

Hans: "Yes, very often."
I: "Does it make a loud row when it does lumf?"
Hans: "Yes."
I: "What does the row remind you of?"
Hans: "Like when lumf falls into the chamber."

"The bus-horse that falls down and makes a row with its feet is no doubt—a lumf falling and making a noise. His fear of defaecation and his fear of heavily loaded carts is equivalent to the fear of a heavily loaded stomach."

In this roundabout way Hans's father was beginning to get a glimmering of the true state of affairs.

"April 11th. At luncheon Hans said: 'If only we had a bath at Gmunden, so that I didn't have to go to the public baths!' It is a fact that at Gmunden he was always taken to the neighbouring public baths to be given his warm

[27] "Hans's mother gives him his bath."
[28] "To take it away to be repaired."

bath—a proceeding against which he used to protest with passionate tears. And in Vienna, too, he always screams if he is made to sit or lie in the big bath. He must be given his bath kneeling or standing."

Hans was now beginning to bring fuel to the analysis in the shape of spontaneous utterances of his own. This remark of his established the connection between his two last phantasies—that of the plumber who unscrewed the bath and that of the unsuccessful journey to Gmunden. His father had correctly inferred from the latter that Hans had some aversion to Gmunden. This, by the way, is another good reminder of the fact that what emerges from the unconscious is to be understood in the light not of what goes before but of what comes after.

"I asked him whether he was afraid, and if so of what.

Hans: "Because of falling in."

I: "But why were you never afraid when you had your bath in the little bath?"

Hans: "Why, I sat in that one. I couldn't lie down in it, it was too small."

I: "When you went in a boat at Gmunden weren't you afraid of falling into the water?"

Hans: "No, because I held on, so I couldn't fall in. It's only in the big bath that I'm afraid of falling in."

I: "But Mamma baths you in it. Are you afraid of Mummy dropping you in the water?"

Hans: "I'm afraid of her letting go and my head going in."

I: "But you know Mummy's fond of you and won't let go of you."

Hans: "I only just thought it."

I: "Why?"

Hans: "I don't know at all."

I: "Perhaps it was because you'd been naughty and thought she didn't love you any more?"

Hans: "Yes."

I: "When you were watching Mummy giving Hanna her

bath, perhaps you wished she would let go of her so that Hanna should fall in?"

Hans: "Yes."

Hans's father, we cannot help thinking, had made a very good guess.

"April 12th. As we were coming back from Lainz in a second-class carriage, Hans looked at the black leather upholstery of the seats, and said: 'Ugh! that makes me spit! Black drawers and black horses make me spit too, because I have to do lumf.'

I: "Perhaps you saw something of Mummy's that was black, and it frightened you?"

Hans: "Yes."

I: "Well, what was it?"

Hans: "I don't know. A black blouse or black stockings."

I: "Perhaps it was black hair near her widdler, when you were curious and looked."

Hans (defending himself): "But I didn't see her widdler."

"Another time, he was once more frightened at a cart driving out of the yard gates opposite. 'Don't the gates look like a behind?' I asked.

He: "And the horses are the lumfs!" Since then, whenever he sees a cart driving out, he says: "Look, there's a 'lumfy' coming!" This form of the word ("lumfy") is quite a new one to him; it sounds like a term of endearment. My sister-in-law always calls her child "Wumfy."

"On April 13th he saw a piece of liver in the soup and exclaimed: 'Ugh! A lumf!' Meat croquettes, too, he eats with evident reluctance, because their form and colour remind him of lumf.

"In the evening my wife told me that Hans had been put out on the balcony and had said: 'I thought to myself Hanna was on the balcony and fell down off it.' I had once or twice told him to be careful that Hanna did not get too near the balustrade when she was out on the balcony; for the railing was designed in the most unpractical way (by a Secessionist craftsman) and had big gaps in it which I had to have filled in with wire netting. Hans's repressed wish was very transparent. His mother asked him if he would rather Hanna were not there, to which he said 'Yes.'

"April 14th. The theme of Hanna is uppermost. As you may remember from earlier records, Hans felt a strong aversion to the new-born baby that robbed him of a part of his parents' love. This dislike has not entirely disappeared and is only partly over-compensated by an exaggerated affection.[29] He has already several times expressed a wish that the stork should bring no more babies and that we should pay him money not to bring any more *out of the big box* where babies are. (Compare his fear of furniture-vans. Does not a bus look like a big box?) Hanna screams such a lot, he says, and that's a nuisance to him.

"Once he suddenly said: 'Can you remember when Hanna came? She lay beside Mummy in bed, so nice and good.' (His praise rang suspiciously hollow.)

"And then as regards downstairs, outside the house. There is again great progress to be reported. Even drays cause him less alarm. Once he called out, almost with joy: 'Here comes a horse with something black on its mouth!' And I was at last able to establish the fact that it was a horse with a leather muzzle. But Hans was not in the least afraid of this horse.

"Once he knocked on the pavement with his stick and said: 'I say, is there a man underneath?—some one buried?—or is that only in the cemetery?' So he is occupied not only with the riddle of life but with the riddle of death.

---

[29] The "Hanna" theme immediately succeeded the "lumf" theme, and the explanation of this at length begins to dawn upon us: Hanna was a lumf herself—babies were lumfs.

"When we got indoors again I saw a box standing in the front hall, and Hans said: 'Hanna travelled with us to Gmunden in a box like that. Whenever we travelled to Gmunden she travelled with us in the box. You don't believe me again? Really, Daddy. Do believe me. We got a big box and it was full of babies; they sat in the bath.' (A small bath had been packed inside the box.) 'I put them in it. Really and truly. I can remember quite well.'[30]

I: "What can you remember?"

Hans: "That Hanna travelled in the box; because I haven't forgotten about it. My word of honour!"

I: "But last year Hanna travelled with us in the railway carriage."

Hans: "But before that she always travelled with us in the box."

I: "Didn't Mummy have the box?"

Hans: "Yes. Mummy had it."

I: "Where?"

Hans: "At home in the attic."

I: "Perhaps she carried it about with her?"[31]

Hans: "No. And when we travel to Gmunden this time Hanna 'll travel in the box again."

I: "And how did she get out of the box, then?"

Hans: "She was taken out."

I: "By Mummy?"

Hans: "Mummy and me. Then we got into the carriage, and Hanna rode on the horse, and the coachman said 'Gee-up.' The coachman sat up in front. Were you there

---

[30] Hans was now going off into a phantasy. We see that a box and a bath have the same meaning for him, that they both represent the space which contains the babies. Let us bear in mind Hans's repeated assurances on this point.

[31] The box was of course the womb. Hans's father was trying to let him know that he understood this. And the same is true of the caskets in which so many of the heroes of mythology were exposed, from the time of King Sargon of Agade onwards.—(*Additional Note*, 1923.) Cf. Rank's study, *Der Mythus von der Geburt des Helden*, 1909.

too? Mummy knows all about it. Mummy doesn't know; she's forgotten about it already, but don't tell her anything!"

"I made him repeat the whole of this.

Hans: "Then Hanna got out."
I: "Why, she couldn't walk at all then."
Hans: "Well then, we lifted her down."
I: "But how could she have sat on the horse? She couldn't sit up at all last year."
Hans: "Oh yes, she sat up all right, and called out 'Gee-up,' and whipped with her whip—'Gee-up! Gee-up!' —the whip I used to have. The horse hadn't any stirrups, but Hanna rode it. I'm not joking, you know, Daddy."

What can be the meaning of the boy's obstinate persistence in all this nonsense? Oh no, it was no nonsense: it was parody, it was Hans's revenge upon his father. It was as much as to say: *"If you really expect me to believe that the stork brought Hanna in October, when even in the summer, while we were travelling to Gmunden, I'd noticed how big mother's stomach was,—then I expect you to believe my lies."* What can be the meaning of the assertion that even the previous summer Hanna had travelled with them to Gmunden "in the box," except that he knew about his mother's pregnancy? His holding out the prospect of a repetition of this journey in the box in each successive year exemplifies a common way in which unconscious thoughts from the past emerge into consciousness; or it may have special reasons and express his dread of seeing a similar pregnancy repeated on their next summer holiday. We now see, moreover, what the circumstances were that had made him take a dislike to the journey to Gmunden, as his second phantasy had indicated.

"Later on, I asked him how Hanna had actually come into his mother's bed after she was born."

This gave Hans a chance of letting himself go and fairly "stuffing" his father.

Hans: "Hanna just came. Frau Kraus" (the midwife) "put her in the bed. She couldn't walk, of course. But the stork carried her in his beak. Of course she couldn't walk." (He went on without a pause.) "The stork came up the stairs up to the landing, and then he knocked and everybody was asleep, and he had the right key and unlocked the door and put Hanna in *your*[32] bed, and Mummy was asleep—no, the stork put her in *her* bed. It was the middle of the night, and then the stork put her in the bed very quietly, he didn't trample about at all, and then he took his hat and went away again. No, he hadn't got a hat."

I: "Who took his hat? The doctor, perhaps?"

Hans: "Then the stork went away; he went home, and then he rang at the door, and every one in the house stopped sleeping. But don't tell this to Mummy or Tini" (the cook). "It's a secret."

I: "Are you fond of Hanna?"

Hans: "Oh yes, very fond."

I: "Would you rather that Hanna weren't alive or that she were?"

Hans: "I'd rather she weren't alive."

I: "Why?"

Hans: "At any rate she wouldn't scream so, and I can't bear her screaming."

I: "Why, you scream yourself."

Hans: "But Hanna screams too."

I: "Why can't you bear it?"

Hans: "Because she screams so loud."

I: "Why, she doesn't scream at all."

Hans: "When she's whacked on her bare bottom, then she screams."

I: "Have you ever whacked her?"

Hans: "When Mummy whacks her on her bottom, then she screams."

I: "And you don't like that?"

[32] Ironical, of course. Like his subsequent request that none of the secret should be betrayed to his mother.

Hans: "No. . . . Why? Because she makes such a row with her screaming."

I: "If you'd rather she weren't alive, you can't be fond of her at all."

Hans (assenting): "H'm, well."

I: "That was why you thought when Mummy was giving her her bath, if only she'd let go, Hanna would fall into the water . . ."

Hans (taking me up): ". . . and die."

I: "And then you'd be alone with Mummy. A good boy doesn't wish that sort of thing, though."

Hans: "But he may think it."

I: "But that isn't good."

Hans: "If he thinks it, it is good all the same, because you can write it to the Professor."[33]

"Later on I said to him: 'You know, when Hanna gets bigger and can talk, you'll be fonder of her.'

Hans: "Oh no. I *am* fond of her. In the autumn, when she's big, I shall go with her to the Stadtpark quite alone, and explain everything to her."

"As I was beginning to give him some further enlightenment, he interrupted me, probably with the intention of explaining to me that it was not so wicked of him to wish that Hanna was dead.

Hans: "You know, all the same, she'd been alive a long time even before she was here. When she was with the stork she was alive too."

I: "No. Perhaps she wasn't with the stork after all."

Hans: "Who brought her, then? The stork had got her."

I: "Where did he bring her from, then?"

Hans: "Oh—from him."

I: "Where had he got her, then?"

Hans: "In the box; in the *stork-box*."

I: "Well, and what does the box look like?"

Hans: "Red. Painted red." (Blood?)

I: "Who told you that?"

[33] Well done, little Hans! I could wish for no better understanding of psychoanalysis from any grown-up.

A PHOBIA IN A FIVE YEAR-OLD / 113

Hans: "Mummy . . . I thought it to myself . . . it's in the book."

I: "In what book?"

Hans: "In the picture-book." (I made him fetch his first picture-book. In it was a picture of a stork's nest with storks, on a red chimney. This was the box. Curiously enough, on the same page there was also a picture of a horse being shod.[34] Hans had transferred the babies into the box, as they were not to be seen in the nest.)

I: "And what did the stork do with her?"

Hans: "Then the stork brought Hanna here. In his beak. You know, the stork that's at Schönbrunn, and that bit the umbrella." (A reminiscence of an episode at Schönbrunn.)

I: "Did you see how the stork brought Hanna?"

Hans: "Why, I was still asleep, you know. A stork can never bring a little girl or a little boy in the morning."

I: "Why?"

Hans: "He can't. A stork can't do it. Do you know why? So that people shan't see. And then, all at once, in the morning, there's a little girl there."[35]

I: "But, all the same, you were curious at the time to know how the stork did it?"

Hans: "Oh yes."

I: "What did Hanna look like when she came?"

Hans (hypocritically): "All white and lovely. So pretty."

[34] [In view of what follows presently it may be worth remarking that the German word for "shod" (*"beschlagen"*) differs in only a single letter from that for "beaten" (*"geschlagen"*).—*Trans.*]

[35] There is no need to find fault with Hans's inconsistencies. In the previous conversation his disbelief in the stork had emerged from his unconscious and had been coupled with the exasperation he felt against his father for making so many mysteries. But he had now become calmer and was answering his father's questions with official thoughts in which he had worked out glosses upon the many difficulties involved in the stork hypothesis.

I: "But when you saw her the first time you didn't like her."

Hans: "Oh, I did; very much!"

I: "You were surprised that she was so small, though."

Hans: "Yes."

I: "How small was she?"

Hans: "Like a baby stork."

I: "Like what else? Like a lumf, perhaps?"

Hans: "Oh no. A lumf's much bigger . . . a bit smaller than Hanna, really."

I had predicted to his father that it would be possible to trace back Hans's phobia to thoughts and wishes occasioned by the birth of his baby sister. But I had omitted to point out that according to the sexual theory of children a baby is a "lumf," so that Hans's path would lie through the excremental complex. It was owing to this neglect on my part that the progress of the case became temporarily obscured. Now that the matter had been cleared up, Hans's father attempted to examine the boy a second time upon this important point.

The next day, "I got Hans to repeat what he had told me yesterday. He said: 'Hanna travelled to Gmunden in the big box, and Mummy travelled in the railway carriage, and Hanna travelled in the luggage train with the box; and then when we got to Gmunden Mummy and I lifted Hanna out and put her on the horse. The coachman sat up in front, and Hanna had the old whip' (the whip he had last year) 'and whipped the horse and kept on saying "Gee-up," and it was such fun, and the coachman whipped too.—The coachman didn't whip at all, because Hanna had the whip.—The coachman had the reins—Hanna had the reins too.' (On each occasion we drove in a carriage from the station to the house. Hans was here trying to reconcile fact and fancy.) 'At Gmunden we lifted Hanna down from the horse, and she walked up the steps by herself.' (Last year, when Hanna was at Gmunden, she was eight months old. The year before that—and Hans's phantasy evidently relates to that time—his mother had been five months gone with child when we arrived at Gmunden.)

I: "*Last* year Hanna was there."

Hans: "Last year she drove in the carriage; but the year before that, when she was living with us . . ."

I: "Was she with us already then?"

Hans: "Yes. You were always there; you used always to go in the boat with me, and Anna was our servant."

I: "But that wasn't last year. Hanna wasn't alive then."

Hans: "*Yes, she was alive then.* Even while she was still travelling in the box she could run about and she could say 'Anna.' " (She has only been able to do so for the last four months.)

I: "But she wasn't with us at all then."

Hans: "Oh yes, she was; she was with the stork."

I: "How old is she, then?"

Hans: "She'll be two years old in the autumn. Hanna *was* there, you know she was."

I: "And when was she with the stork in the stork-box?"

Hans: "A long time before she travelled in the box, a very long time."

I: "How long has Hanna been able to walk, then? When she was at Gmunden she couldn't walk yet."

Hans: "Not last year; but else she could."

I: "But Hanna's only been at Gmunden once."

Hans: "No. She's been twice. Yes, that's it. I can remember quite well. Ask Mummy, she'll tell you soon enough."

I: "It's not true, all the same."

Hans: "Yes, it *is* true. *When she was at Gmunden the first time she could walk and ride, and later on she had to be carried.*—No. It was only later on that she rode, and last year she had to be carried."

I: "But it's only quite a short time that she's been walking. At Gmunden she couldn't walk."

Hans: "Yes. Just you write it down. I can remember quite well.—Why are you laughing?"

I: "Because you're a fraud; because you know quite well that Hanna's only been at Gmunden once."

Hans: "No, that isn't true. The first time she rode on the horse . . . and the second time . . ." (He showed signs of evident uncertainty.)

I: "Perhaps the horse was Mummy?"

Hans: "No, a real horse in a fly."

I: "But we used always to have a carriage with two horses."

Hans: "Well, then, it was a carriage and pair."

I: "What did Hanna eat inside the box?"

Hans: "They put in bread-and-butter for her, and herring, and radishes" (the sort of things we used to have for supper at Gmunden), "and as Hanna went along she buttered her bread-and-butter and ate fifty meals."

I: "Didn't Hanna scream?"

Hans: "No."

I: "What did she do, then?"

Hans: "Sat quite still inside."

I: "Didn't she push about?"

Hans: "No, she kept on eating all the time and didn't stir once. She drank up two big mugs of coffee—by the morning it was all gone, and she left the bits behind in the box, the leaves of the two radishes and a knife for cutting the radishes. She gobbled everything up like a hare: one minute and it was all finished. It *was* a joke. Hanna and I really travelled together in the box; I slept the whole night in the box." (We did in fact, two years ago, make the journey to Gmunden by night.) "And Mummy travelled in the railway carriage. And we kept on eating all the time when we were driving in the carriage, too; it *was* ripping. —She didn't ride on a horse at all . . ." (he now became undecided, for he knew that we had driven with two horses) ". . . she sat in the carriage. Yes, that's how it was, but Hanna and I drove quite by ourselves . . . Mummy rode on the horse, and Karoline" (our maid last year) "on the other . . . I say, what I'm telling you isn't a bit true."

I: "What isn't true?"

Hans: "None of it is. I say, let's put Hanna and me in

the box[36] and I'll widdle into the box. I'll just widdle into my knickers; I don't care a bit; there's nothing at all shameful in it. I say, that isn't a joke, you know; but it's great fun, though."

"Then he told me the story of how the stork came—the same story as yesterday, except that he left out the part about the stork taking his hat when he went away.

I: "Where did the stork keep his latch-key?"
Hans: "In his pocket."
I: "And where's the stork's pocket?"
Hans: "In his beak."
I: "It's in his beak! I've never seen a stork yet with a key in his beak."
Hans: "How else could he have got in? How did the stork come in at the door, then? No, it isn't true; I just made a mistake. The stork rang at the front door and some one let him in."
I: "And how did he ring?"
Hans: "He rang the bell."
I: "How did he do that?"
Hans: "He took his beak and pressed on it with his beak."
I: "And did he shut the door again?"
Hans: "No, a maid shut it. She was up already, you see, and opened the door for him and shut it."
I: "Where does the stork live?"
Hans: "Where? In the box where he keeps the little girls. At Schönbrunn, perhaps."
I: "I've never seen a box at Schönbrunn."
Hans: "It must be farther off, then.—Do you know how the stork opens the box? He takes his beak—the box has got a key, too—he takes his beak, lifts up one" (*i.e.* one-half of the beak) "and unlocks it like this." (He demonstrated the process on the lock of the writing-table.) "This is a handle too."

[36] "The box standing in the front hall which we had taken as luggage to Gmunden."

I: "Isn't a little girl like that too heavy for him?"

Hans: "Oh no."

I: "I say, doesn't a bus look like a stork-box?"

Hans: "Yes."

I: "And a furniture-waggon?"

Hans: "And a scallywaggon" ("scallywag"—a term of abuse for naughty children) "too."

"April 17th. Yesterday Hans carried out his long pre-meditated scheme of going across into the courtyard opposite. He would not do it to-day, as there was a cart standing at the loading dock exactly opposite the entrance gates. "When a cart stands there," he said to me, "I'm afraid I shall tease the horses and they'll fall down and make a row with their feet."

I: "How does one tease horses?"

Hans: "When you're cross with them you tease them, and when you shout 'Gee-up.' "[37]

I: "Have you ever teased horses?"

Hans: "Yes, quite often. I'm *afraid* I shall do it, but I don't *really*."

I: "Did you ever tease horses at Gmunden?"

Hans: "No."

I: "But you like teasing them?"

Hans: "Oh yes, very much."

I: "Would you like to whip them?"

Hans: "Yes."

I: "Would you like to beat the horses as Mummy beats Hanna? You like that too, you know."

Hans: "It doesn't do the horses any harm when they're beaten." (I said this to him once to mitigate his fear of see-ing horses whipped.) "Once I really did it. Once I had the whip and whipped the horse, and it fell down and made a row with its feet."

I: "When?"

---

[37] "Hans has often been very much terrified when drivers beat their horses and shout 'Gee-up.' "

Hans: "At Gmunden."

I: "A real horse? Harnessed to a cart?"

Hans: "It wasn't in the cart."

I: "Where was it, then?"

Hans: "I just held it so that it shouldn't run away." (Of course all this sounded most improbable.)

I: "Where was that?"

Hans: "Near the trough."

I: "Who let you? Had the coachman left the horse standing there?"

Hans: "It was just a horse from the stables."

I: "How did it get to the trough?"

Hans: "I took it there."

I: "Where from? Out of the stables?"

Hans: "I took it out because I wanted to beat it."

I: "Was there no one in the stables?"

Hans: "Oh yes, Loisl." (The coachman at Gmunden.)

I: "Did he let you?"

Hans: "I talked nicely to him, and he said I might do it."

I: "What did you say to him?"

Hans: "Could I take the horse and whip it and shout at it. And he said 'Yes.' "

I: "Did you whip it a lot?"

Hans: "What I've told you isn't the least true."

I: "How much of it's true?"

Hans: "None of it's true; I only told it you for fun."

I: "You never took a horse out of the stables?"

Hans: "Oh no."

I: "But you wanted to."

Hans: "Oh yes, wanted to. I've thought it to myself."

I: "At Gmunden?"

Hans: "No, only here. I thought it in the morning when I was quite undressed; no, in the morning in bed."

I: "Why did you never tell me about it?"

Hans: "I didn't think of it."

I: "You thought it to yourself because you saw it in the street."

Hans: "Yes."

I: "Which would you really like to beat? Mummy, Hanna, or me?"

Hans: "Mummy."

I: "Why?"

Hans: "I should just like to beat her."

I: "When did you ever see any one beating their Mummy?"

Hans: "I've never seen any one do it, never in all my life."

I: "And yet you'd just like to do it. How would you like to set about it?"

Hans: "With a carpet-beater." (His mother often threatens to beat him with the carpet-beater.)

"I was obliged to break off the conversation for to-day.

"In the street Hans explained to me that buses, furniture-vans, and coal-carts were stork-box carts."

That is to say, pregnant women. Hans's access of sadism immediately before cannot be unconnected with the present theme.

"April 21st. This morning Hans said that he had thought as follows: 'There was a train at Lainz and I travelled with my Lainz Grandmamma to the Hauptzollamt station. You hadn't got down from the bridge yet, and the second train was already at St. Veit.[38] When you came down, the train was there already, and we got in.'

"(Hans was at Lainz yesterday. In order to get on to the departure platform one has to cross a bridge. From the platform one can see along the line as far as St. Veit station. The whole thing is a trifle obscure. Hans's original thought had no doubt been that he had gone off by the first train, which I had missed, and that then a second train had come in from Unter St. Veit and that I had gone after him in it. But he had distorted a part of this runaway

[38] [Unter St. Veit is the next station to Lainz in the direction away from Vienna.—*Trans.*]

phantasy, so that he said finally: 'Both of us only got away by the second train.'

"This phantasy is related to the last one, which was not interpreted, and according to which we took too long to put on our clothes in the station at Gmunden, so that the train carried us on.)

"Afternoon, in front of the house. Hans suddenly ran indoors as a carriage with two horses came along. I could see nothing unusual about it, and asked him what was wrong. 'The horses are so proud,' he said, 'that I'm afraid they'll fall down.' (The coachman was reining the horses in tight, so that they were trotting with short steps and holding their heads high. In fact their action *was* 'proud.')

"I asked him who it really was that was so proud.

He: "You are, when I come into bed with Mummy."

I: "So you want me to fall down?"

Hans: "Yes. You've got to be naked" (meaning "barefoot," as Fritzl had been) "and knock up against a stone, and blood must flow, and then I'll be able to be alone with Mummy for a little bit at all events. When you come up into our flat I'll be able to run away quick so that you don't see."

I: "Can you remember who it was that knocked up against the stone?"

He: "Yes, Fritzl."

I: "When Fritzl fell down, what did you think?"[39]

He: "That you should hit the stone and tumble down."

I: "So you'd like to go to Mummy?"

He: "Yes."

I: "What do I really scold you for?"

He: "I don't know." (!!)

I: "Why?"

He: "Because you're cross."

I: "But that's not true."

[39] "So that in fact Fritzl did fall down—which he at one time denied."

Hans: "Yes, it *is* true. You're cross. I know you are. It must be true."

"Evidently, therefore, my explanation that only *little* boys come into bed with their Mummies and that *big* ones sleep in their own beds had not impressed him very much.

"I suspect that his desire to 'tease' the horse, *i.e.* to beat it and shout at it, does not apply to his mother, as he pretended, but to me. No doubt he only put her forward because he was unwilling to admit the alternative to me. For the last few days he has been particularly affectionate to me."

Speaking with the air of superiority which is so easily acquired after the event, we may correct Hans's father, and explain that the boy's wish to "tease" the horse had two constituents; it was compounded of an obscure sadistic desire for his mother and of a clear impulse for revenge against his father. The latter could not be reproduced until the former's turn had come to emerge in connection with the pregnancy complex. In the process of the formation of a phobia from the unconscious thoughts underlying it condensation takes place; and for that reason the course of the analysis can never follow that of the development of the neurosis.

"April 22nd. This morning Hans again thought something to himself: 'A street-boy was riding on a truck, and the guard came and undressed the boy quite naked and made him stand there till next morning, and in the morning the boy gave the guard 50,000 florins so that he could go on riding on the truck.'

"(The Nordbahn[40] runs past opposite our house. In a siding there stood a trolley on which Hans once saw a street-boy riding. He wanted to do so too; but I told him it was not allowed, and that if he did the guard would be after him. A second element in this phantasy is Hans's repressed wish to be naked.)"

[40] [Northern Railway.]

It has been noticeable for some time that Hans's imagination was being coloured by images derived from traffic,[41] and was advancing systematically from horses, which draw vehicles, to railways. In the same way a railway-phobia eventually becomes associated with every street-phobia.

"At lunch-time I was told that Hans *had been playing all the morning with an india-rubber doll which he called Grete. He had pushed a small penknife in through the opening to which the little tin squeaker had originally been attached, and had then torn the doll's legs apart so as to let the knife drop out. He had said to the nurse-maid, pointing between the doll's legs: 'Look, there's its widdler!'*

I: "What was it you were playing at with your doll to-day?"

Hans: "I tore its legs apart. Do you know why? Because there was a knife inside it belonging to Mummy. I put it in at the place where its head squeaks, and then I tore apart its legs and it came out there."

I: "Why did you tear its legs apart? So that you could see its widdler?"

He: "Its widdler was there before; I could have seen it anyhow."

I: "What did you put the knife in for?"

He: "I don't know."

I: "Well, what does the knife look like?"

He brought it to me.

I: "Did you think it was a baby, perhaps?"

He: "No, I didn't think anything at all; but I believe the stork got a baby once—or some one."

I: "When?"

He: "Once. I heard so—or didn't I hear it at all?—or did I say it wrong?"

I: "What does 'say it wrong' mean?"

He: "That it's not true."

[41] Moreover, a "station" is used for purposes of *"Verkehr"* ["traffic," "intercourse," "sexual intercourse"]: this affords the psychological wrappings in many cases of railway phobia.

I: "Everything one says is a bit true."

He: "Well, yes, a little bit."

I (after changing the subject): "How do you think chickens are born?"

He: "The stork just makes them grow; the stork makes chickens grow—no, God does."

"I explained to him that chickens lay eggs, and that out of the eggs there come other chickens.

Hans laughed.

I: "Why do you laugh?"

He: "Because I like what you've told me."

He said he had seen it happen already.

I: "Where?"

Hans: "You did it."

I: "Where did I lay an egg?"

Hans: "At Gmunden; you laid an egg in the grass, and all at once a chicken came hopping out. You laid an egg once; I know you did, I know it for certain. Because Mummy said so."

I: "I'll ask Mummy if that's true."

Hans: "It isn't true a bit. But *I* once laid an egg, and a chicken came hopping out."

I: "Where?"

Hans: "At Gmunden I lay down in the grass—no, I knelt down—and the children didn't look on at me, and all at once in the morning I said: 'Look for it, children; I laid an egg yesterday.' And all at once they looked, and all at once they saw an egg, and out of it there came a little Hans. Well, what are you laughing for? Mummy didn't know about it, and Karoline didn't know, because no one was looking on, and all at once I laid an egg, and all at once it was there. Really and truly. Daddy, when does a chicken grow out of an egg? When it's left alone? Must it be eaten?"

"I explained the matter to him.

Hans: "All right, let's leave it with the hen; then a chicken'll grow. Let's pack it up in the box and let's take it to Gmunden."

As his parents still hesitated to give him the information which was already long overdue, little Hans had by a bold stroke taken the conduct of the analysis into his own hands. By means of a brilliant symptomatic act, *"Look!"* he had said to them, *"this is how I imagine that a birth takes place."* What he had told the maid-servant about the meaning of his game with the doll had been insincere; to his father he explicitly denied that he had only wanted to see its widdler. After his father had told him, as a kind of payment on account, how chickens come out of eggs, Hans gave a combined expression to his dissatisfaction, his mistrust, and his superior knowledge in a charming piece of persiflage, which culminated with his last words in an unmistakable allusion to his sister's birth.

I: "What were you playing at with your doll?"

Hans: "I said 'Grete' to her."

I: "Why?"

Hans: "Because I said 'Grete' to her."

I: "How did you play?"

Hans: "I just looked after her like a real baby."

I: "Would you like to have a little girl?"

Hans: "Oh yes. Why not? I should like to have one, but Mummy mustn't have one; I don't like that."

"(He has often expressed this view before. He is afraid of losing still more of his position if a third child arrives.)

I: "But only women have children."

Hans: "I'm going to have a little girl."

I: "Where will you get her, then?"

Hans: "Why, from the stork. *He takes the little girl out,* and all at once the little girl lays an egg, and out of the egg there comes another Hanna—another Hanna. Out of Hanna there comes another Hanna. No, *one* Hanna comes out."

I: "You'd like to have a little girl."

Hans: "Yes, *the next year I'm going to have one,* and she'll be called Hanna too."

I: "But why isn't Mummy to have a little girl?"

Hans: "Because *I* want to have a little girl for once."

I: "But you can't have a little girl."

Hans: "Oh yes, boys have girls and girls have boys."[42]

I: "Boys don't have children. Only women, only Mummies have children."

Hans: "But why shouldn't I?"

I: "Because God's arranged it like that."

Hans: "But why don't *you* have one? Oh yes, you'll have one all right. Just you wait."

I: "I shall have to wait some time."

Hans: "But I belong to you."

I: "But Mummy brought you into the world. So you belong to Mummy and me."

Hans: "Does Hanna belong to me or to Mummy?"

I: "To Mummy."

Hans: "No, to me. *Why not to me and Mummy?*"

I: "Hanna belongs to me, Mummy, and you."

Hans: "There you are, you see."

So long as the child is in ignorance of the female genitals, there is naturally a vital gap in his comprehension of sexual matters.

"On April 24th my wife and I enlightened Hans up to a certain point: we told him that children grow inside their Mummy, and are then brought into the world by being pressed out of her like a 'lumf,' and that this involves a great deal of pain.

"In the afternoon we went out in front of the house. There was a visible improvement in his state. He ran after carts, and the only thing that betrayed a remaining trace of his anxiety was the fact that he did not venture away from the neighbourhood of the street-door and could not be induced to go for any considerable walk.

"On April 25th Hans butted me in the stomach with his head, as he has already done once before. I asked him if he was a goat.

---

[42] Here is another bit of infantile sexual theory with an unsuspected meaning.

" 'Yes,' he said, 'a ram.' I inquired where he had seen a ram.

He: "At Gmunden: Fritzl had one." (Fritzl had a real lamb to play with.)

I: "You must tell me about the lamb. What did it do?"

Hans: "You know, Fräulein Mizzi" (a schoolmistress who lived in the house) "used always to put Hanna on the lamb, but it couldn't stand up then and it couldn't butt. If you went up to it it used to butt, because it had horns. Fritzl used to lead it on a string and tie it to a tree. He always tied it to a tree."

I: "Did the lamb butt you?"

Hans: "It jumped up at me; Fritzl took me up to it once. . . . I went up to it once and didn't know, and all at once it jumped up at me. It was such fun—I wasn't frightened."

"This was certainly untrue.

I: "Are you fond of Daddy?"

Hans: "Oh yes."

I: "Or perhaps not."

Hans was playing with a little toy horse. At that moment the horse fell down, and Hans shouted out: "The horse has fallen down! Look what a row it's making!"

I: "You're a little vexed with Daddy because Mummy's fond of him."

Hans: "No."

I: "Then why do you always cry whenever Mummy gives me a kiss? It's because you're jealous."

Hans: "Jealous, yes."

I: "You'd like to be Daddy yourself."

Hans: "Oh yes."

I: "What would you like to do if you were Daddy?"

Hans: "And you were Hans? I'd like to take you to Lainz every Sunday—no, every week-day too. If I were Daddy I'd be ever so nice and good."

I: "But what would you like to do with Mummy?"

Hans: "Take her to Lainz, too."

I: "And what besides?"

Hans: "Nothing."

I: "Then why were you jealous?"

Hans: "I don't know."

I: "Were you jealous at Gmunden, too?"

Hans: "Not at Gmunden." (This is not true.) "At Gmunden I had my own things. I had a garden at Gmunden and children too."

I: "Can you remember how the cow got a calf?"

Hans: "Oh yes. It came in a cart." (No doubt he had been told this at Gmunden; another sally against the stork theory.) "And another cow pressed it out of its behind." (This was already the fruit of his enlightenment, which he was trying to bring into harmony with the cart theory.)

I: "It isn't true that it came in a cart; it came out of the cow in the cow-shed."

"Hans disputed this, saying that he had seen the cart in the morning. I pointed out to him that he had probably been told this about the calf having come in a cart. In the end he admitted this, and said 'Most likely Berta told me, or not—or perhaps it was the landlord. He was there and it was at night, so it *is* true after all, what I've been telling you—or it seems to me nobody told me; I thought it to myself in the night.'

"Unless I am mistaken, the calf was taken away in a cart; hence the confusion.

I: "Why didn't you think it was the stork that brought it?"

Hans: "I didn't want to think that."

I: "But you thought the stork brought Hanna?"

Hans: "In the morning" (of the confinement) "I thought so.—I say, Daddy, was Herr Reisenbichler" (our landlord) "there when the calf came out of the cow?"[43]

I: "I don't know. Do you think he was?"

Hans: "I think so. . . . Daddy, have you noticed now

---

[43] Hans, having good reason to mistrust information given him by grown-up people, was considering whether the landlord might not be more trustworthy than his father.

and then that horses have something black on their mouths?"

I: "I've noticed it now and then in the street at Gmunden."[44]

I: "Did you often get into bed with Mummy at Gmunden?"

Hans: "Yes."

I: "And you used to think to yourself you were Daddy?"

Hans: "Yes."

I: "And then you felt afraid of Daddy?"

Hans: "You know everything; I didn't know anything."

I: "When Fritzl fell down you thought: 'If only Daddy would fall down like that!' And when the lamb butted you you thought: 'If only it would butt Daddy!' Can you remember the funeral at Gmunden?" (The first funeral that Hans had seen. He often recalls it, and it is no doubt a screen-memory.)

Hans: "Yes. What about it?"

I: "You thought then that if only Daddy were to die you'd be Daddy."

Hans: "Yes."

I: "What carts are you still afraid of?"

Hans: "All of them."

I: "You know that's not true."

Hans: "I'm not afraid of carriages and pair or cabs with one horse. I'm afraid of buses and luggage-carts, but only when they're loaded up, not when they're empty. When there's one horse and the cart's loaded full up, then I'm afraid; but when there are two horses and it's loaded full up, then I'm not afraid."

I: "Are you afraid of buses because there are so many people inside?"

Hans: "Because there's so much luggage on the top."

---

[44] The connection of thought is as follows. For a long time his father had refused to believe what he said about there being something black on horses' mouths, but finally it had been verified.

I: "When Mummy was having Hanna, was she loaded full up too?"

Hans: "Mummy'll be loaded full up again when she has another one, when another one begins to grow, when another one's inside her."

I: "And you'd like that?"

Hans: "Yes."

I: "You said you didn't want Mummy to have another baby."

Hans: "Well, then she won't be loaded up again. Mummy said if Mummy didn't want one, God didn't want one either. If Mummy doesn't want one she won't have one." (Hans naturally asked yesterday if there were any more babies inside Mummy. I told him not, and said that if God did not wish it none would grow inside her.)

Hans: "But Mummy told me if *she* didn't want it no more'd grow, and you say if *God* doesn't want it."

"So I told him it was as I had said, upon which he observed: 'You were there, though, weren't you? You know better, for certain." He then proceeded to cross-question his mother, and she reconciled the two statements by declaring that if she didn't want it God didn't want it either.[45]

I: "It seems to me that, all the same, you do wish Mummy would have a baby."

Hans: "But I don't want it to happen."

I: "But you wish for it?"

Hans: "Oh yes, *wish.*"

I: "Do you know why you wish for it? It's because you'd like to be Daddy."

Hans: "Yes. . . . How does it work?"

I: "How does what work?"

Hans: "You say Daddies don't have babies; so how does it work, my wanting to be Daddy?"

I: "You'd like to be Daddy and married to Mummy;

---

[45] Ce que femme veut Dieu veut. But Hans, with his usual acumen, had once more put his finger upon a most serious problem.

you'd like to be as big as me and have a moustache; and you'd like Mummy to have a baby."

Hans: "And, Daddy, when I'm married I'll only have one if I want to, when I'm married to Mummy, and if I don't want a baby, God won't want it either, when I'm married."

I: "Would you like to be married to Mummy?"

Hans: "Oh yes."

It is easy to see that Hans's enjoyment of his phantasy was interfered with by his uncertainty as to the part played by fathers and by his doubts as to whether the begetting of children would be under his control.

"On the evening of the same day, as Hans was being put to bed, he said to me: "I say, d'you know what I'm going to do now? Now I'm going to talk to Grete till ten o'clock; she's in bed with me. My children are always in bed with me. Can you tell me why that is?'—As he was very sleepy already, I promised him that we should write it down next day, and he went to sleep.

"I have already noticed in earlier records that since Hans's return from Gmunden he has constantly been having phantasies about 'his children,' has carried on conversations with them, and so on.[46]

"So on April 26th I asked him why he was always thinking of his children.

Hans: "Why? *Because I should so like to have children; but I don't ever want it; I shouldn't like to have them.*"[47]

---

[46] There is no necessity on this account to assume in Hans the presence of a feminine strain of desire for having children. It was with his mother that Hans had had his most blissful experiences as a child, and he was now repeating them, and himself playing the active part, which was thus necessarily that of mother.

[47] This startling contradiction was one between phantasy and reality, between wishing and having. Hans knew that in reality he was a child and that the other children would only

I: "Have you always imagined that Berta and Olga and the rest were your children?"

Hans: "Yes. Franzl, and Fritzl, and Paul too" (his playmates at Lainz), "and Lodi." This is an invented girl's name, that of his favourite child, whom he speaks of most often.—I may here emphasize the fact that the figure of Lodi is not an invention of the last few days, but existed before the date of his receiving the latest piece of enlightenment (April 24th).

I: "Who is Lodi? Is she at Gmunden?"

Hans: "No."

I: "Is there a Lodi?"

Hans: "Yes, I know her."

I: "Who is she, then?"

Hans: "The one I've got here."

I: "What does she look like?"

Hans: "Look like? Black eyes, black hair. . . . I met her once with Mariedl" (at Gmunden) "as I was going into the town."

"When I went into the matter it turned out that this was an invention.[48]

I: "So you thought you were their Mummy?"

Hans: "And so I was their Mummy."

I: "What did you do with your children?"

Hans: "I had them to sleep with me, the girls and the boys."

I: "Every day?"

Hans: "Why, of course."

I: "Did you talk to them?"

Hans: "When I couldn't get all the children into the bed, I put some of the children on the sofa, and some in

---

be in his way; but in phantasy he was a mother and wanted children with whom he could repeat the endearments that he had himself experienced.

[48] It is possible, however, that Hans had exalted into his ideal some one whom he had met casually at Gmunden. The colour of this ideal's eyes and hair, by the way, was copied from his mother.

the pram, and if there were still some left over I took them up to the attic and put them in the box, and if there were any more I put them in the other box."

I: "So the stork-baby-boxes were in the attic?"

Hans: "Yes."

I: "When did you get your children? Was Hanna alive already?"

Hans: "Yes, she had been a long time."

I: "But who did you think you'd got the children from?"

Hans: "Why, from me."[49]

I: "But at that time you hadn't any idea that children came from some one."

Hans: "I thought the stork had brought them." (Clearly a lie and an evasion.)[50]

I: "You had Grete in bed with you yesterday, but you know quite well that boys can't have children."

Hans: "Well, yes. But I believe they can, all the same."

I: "How did you hit upon the name Lodi? No girl's called that. Lotti, perhaps?"

Hans: "Oh no, Lodi. I don't know; but it's a beautiful name, all the same."

I (jokingly): "Perhaps you mean a Schokolodi?"[51]

Hans (promptly): "No, a Saffalodi,[52] . . . because I like eating sausages so much, and salami[53] too."

I: "I say, doesn't a Saffalodi look like a lumf?"

Hans: "Yes."

I: "Well, what does a lumf look like?"

Hans: "Black. You know" (pointing at my eyebrows and moustache), "like this and like this."

[49] Hans could not help answering from the auto-erotic point of view.

[50] They were the children of his phantasy, that is to say, of his onanism.

[51] [*"Schokolade"* is the German for "chocolate."—*Trans.*]

[52] "'Saffaladi' means *'Zervelatwurst'* ['saveloy,' a kind of sausage]. My wife is fond of relating how her aunt always calls it 'Soffilodi.' Hans may have heard this."

[53] [Another kind of sausage.—*Trans.*]

I: "And what else? Round like a Saffaladi?"

Hans: "Yes."

I: "When you sat on the chamber and a lumf came, did you think to yourself you were having a baby?"

Hans (laughing): "Yes. Even at —— Street, and here as well."

I: "You know when the bus-horses fell down? The bus looked like a baby-box, and when the black horse fell down it was just like . . ."

Hans (taking me up): ". . . like having a baby."

I: "And what did you think when it made a row with its feet?"

Hans: "Oh, when I don't want to sit on the chamber and would rather play, then I make a row like this with my feet." (He stamped his feet.)

"This was why he was so much interested in the question whether people *liked* or *did not like* having children.

"All day long to-day Hans has been playing at loading and unloading packing-cases; he said he wished he could have a toy waggon and boxes of that kind to play with. What used most to interest him in the courtyard of the Customs House opposite was the loading and unloading of the carts. And he used to be frightened most when a cart had been loaded up and was on the point of driving off. 'The horses'll fall down,'[54] he used to say. He used to call the doors of the Head Customs House shed 'holes' (thus, the first hole, second hole, third hole, etc.). But now, instead of 'hole," he says 'behind-hole.'

"The anxiety has almost completely disappeared, except that he likes to remain in the neighbourhood of the house, so as to have a line of retreat in case he is frightened. But he never takes flight into the house now, but stops in the street at the time. As we know, his illness began with his turning back in tears while he was out for a walk; and when he was obliged to go for a second walk he only went

---

[54] Do we not use the word *"niederkommen"* [literally, "to come down"] when a woman is delivered?

as far as the Hauptzollamt station on the Stadtbahn, from which our house can still be seen. At the time of my wife's confinement he was of course kept away from her; and his present anxiety, which prevents him from leaving the neighbourhood of the house, is in reality the longing for her which he felt then.

"April 30th. Seeing Hans playing with his imaginary children again, 'Hullo,' I said to him, 'are your children still alive? You know quite well a boy can't have any children.'

Hans: "I know. I was their Mummy before, *now I'm their Daddy.*"

I: "And who's the children's Mummy?"

Hans: "Why, Mummy, and you're their *Grandaddy.*"

I: "So then you'd like to be as big as me, and be married to Mummy, and then you'd like her to have children."

Hans: "Yes, that's what I'd like, and then my Lainz Grandmamma" (my mother) "will be their Grannie."

Things were moving towards a satisfactory conclusion. The little Oedipus had found a happier solution than that prescribed by destiny. Instead of putting his father out of the way, he had granted him the same happiness that he desired himself: he made him a grandfather and let him too marry his own mother.

"On May 1st Hans came to me at lunch-time and said: 'D'you know what? Let's write something down for the Professor."

I: "Well, and what shall it be?"

Hans: "This morning I was in the W.C. with all my children. First I did lumf and widdled, and they looked on. Then I put them on the seat and they widdled and did lumf, and I wiped their behinds with paper. D'you know why? Because I'd so much like to have children; then I'd do everything for them—take them to the W.C., clean their behinds, and do everything one does with children."

After the admission afforded by this phantasy, it will

scarcely be possible to dispute the fact that in Hans's mind there was pleasure attached to the excremental functions.

"In the afternoon he ventured into the Stadtpark for the first time. As it is the First of May, no doubt there was less traffic than usual, but still quite enough to have frightened him up to now. He was very proud of his achievement, and after tea I was obliged to go with him to the Stadtpark once again. On the way we met a bus; Hans pointed it out to me, saying: 'Look! a stork-box cart!' If he goes with me to the Stadtpark again to-morrow, as we have planned, we shall really be able to regard his illness as cured.

"On May 2nd Hans came to me in the morning. 'I say,' he said, 'I thought something to-day.' At first he had forgotten it; but later on he related what follows, though with signs of considerable resistance: *The plumber came; and first he took away my behind with a pair of pincers, and then gave me another, and then the same with my widdler.* He said: "Let me see your behind," and I had to turn round, and he took it away; and then he said: "Let me see your widdler!" ' "

Hans's father grasped the nature of this wish-phantasy, and did not hesitate a moment as to the only interpretation it could bear.

I: "He gave you a *bigger* widdler and a *bigger* behind."

Hans: "Yes."

I: "Like Daddy's; because you'd like to be Daddy."

Hans: "Yes, and I'd like to have a moustache like yours and hairs like yours." (He pointed to the hairs on my chest.)

"In the light of this, we may review the interpretation of Hans's earlier phantasy to the effect that the plumber had come and unscrewed the bath and had stuck a borer into his stomach. The big bath meant a 'behind,' the borer or screwdriver was (as was explained at the time) a widdler.[55]

---

[55] We may perhaps add that the word "borer" was not chosen without regard for its connection with the words "born" and "birth." If so, the child could have made no distinction between "bored" and "born." I accept this suggestion,

The two phantasies are identical. Moreover, a new light is thrown upon Hans's fear of the big bath. (This, by the way, has already diminished.) He dislikes his 'behind' being too small for the big bath."

In the course of the next few days Hans's mother wrote to me several times to express her joy at the little boy's recovery.

A week later came a postscript from Hans's father.

"My dear Professor, I should like to make the following additions to Hans's case history:

"(1) The remission after he had been given his first piece of enlightenment was not so complete as I may have represented it. It is true that Hans went for walks; but only under compulsion and in a state of great anxiety. Once he went with me as far as the Hauptzollamt station, from which our house can still be seen, but could not be induced to go any farther.

"(2) As regards 'raspberry syrup' and 'a gun for shooting with.' Hans is given raspberry syrup when he is constipated. He also frequently confuses the words 'shooting' and 'shitting.'[56]

"(3) Hans was about four years old when he was moved out of our bedroom into a room of his own.

"(4) A trace of his disorder still persists, though it is no longer in the shape of fear but only in that of the normal instinct for asking questions. The questions are mostly concerned with what things are made of (trams, machines, etc.), who makes things, etc. Most of his questions are characterized by the fact that Hans asks them

---

which comes from an experienced fellow-worker, but I am not in a position to say whether we have before us here a deep and universal connection between the two ideas or merely the employment of a verbal coincidence peculiar to German [and English]. Prometheus (Pramantha), the creator of man, is also etymologically "the borer." (Cf. Abraham, *Traum und Mythus,* 1908.)

[56] [In German *"schiessen"* and *"scheissen."*—*Trans.*]

although he has already answered them himself. He only wants to make sure. Once when he had tired me out with his questions and I had said to him: 'Do you think I can answer every question you ask?' he replied: 'Well, I thought as you knew that about the horse you'd know this too.'

"(5) Hans only refers to his illness now as a matter of past history—'at the time when I had my nonsense.'

"(6) An unsolved residue remains behind; for Hans keeps cudgelling his brains to discover what a father has to do with his child, since it is the mother who brings it into the world. This can be seen from his questions, as, for instance: 'I belong to *you*, too, don't I?' (meaning, not only to his mother). It is not clear to him in what way he belongs to me. On the other hand, I have no direct evidence of his having, as you suppose, overheard his parents in the act of coitus.

"(7) In presenting the case one ought perhaps to insist upon the violence of his anxiety. Otherwise it might be said that the boy would have gone out for walks soon enough if he had been given a sound thrashing."

In conclusion let me add these words. With Hans's last phantasy the anxiety which arose from his castration complex was also overcome, and his painful expectations were given a happier turn. Yes, the Doctor (the plumber) *did* come, he *did* take away his penis,—but only to give him a bigger one in exchange for it. For the rest, our young investigator has merely come somewhat early upon the discovery that all knowledge is patchwork, and that each step forward leaves an unsolved residue behind.

3. Epicrisis

I SHALL NOW proceed to examine this observation of the development and resolution of a phobia in a boy under five years of age, and I shall have to do so from three points of view. In the first place I shall consider how far it supports the assertions which I put forward in my *Drei Abhandlungen zur Sexualtheorie* (published in 1905). Secondly, I shall consider to what extent it can contribute towards our understanding of this very frequent form of disorder. And thirdly, I shall consider whether it can be made to shed any light upon the mental life of children or to afford any criticism of our educational aims.

(I)

My impression is that the picture of a child's sexual life presented in this observation of little Hans agrees very well with the account I gave of it (basing my views upon psychoanalytic examinations of adults) in my *Sexualtheorie*. But before going into the details of this agreement I must deal with two objections which will be raised against my making use of the present analysis for this purpose. The first objection is to the effect that Hans was not a normal child, but (as events—the illness itself, in fact—showed) had a predisposition to neurosis, and was a little "degenerate;" it would be illegitimate, therefore, to apply to other, normal children conclusions which might perhaps be true of him. I shall postpone consideration of this objection, since it only limits the value of the observation, and does not completely nullify it. According to the second and more uncompromising objection, an analysis of a child conducted by its father, who went to work instilled with *my* theoretical views and infected with *my* prejudices, must be entirely devoid of any objective worth. A child, it will be said, is necessarily highly suggestible, and in regard to no one, perhaps, more than to its own father; it will allow anything to be forced upon it, out of gratitude to its father for taking so much notice of it; none of its assertions can have any evidential value, and everything it produces in the way of associations, phantasies, and dreams will naturally take the direction into which they are being urged by every possible means. Once more, in short, the whole thing is simply "suggestion"—the only difference being that in the case of a child it can be unmasked much more easily than in that of an adult.

A singular thing. I can remember, when I first began to meddle in the conflict of scientific opinions twenty-two years ago, with what derision the older generation of neurologists and psychiatrists of those days received assertions about suggestion and its effects. Since then the situation has fundamentally changed. The former aversion has been converted into an only too ready acceptance; and this has happened not only as a consequence of the impression which the work of Liébault and Bernheim and their pupils could not fail to create in the course of these two decades, but also because it has since been discovered how great an economy of thought can be effected by the use of the catchword "suggestion." Nobody knows and nobody cares what suggestion is, where it comes from, or when it arises,—it is enough that everything awkward in the region of psychology can be labelled "suggestion." I do not share the view which is at present fashionable that assertions made by children are invariably arbitrary and untrustworthy. The arbitrary has no existence in mental life. The untrustworthiness of the assertions of children is due to the predominance of their imagination, just as the untrustworthiness of the assertions of grown-up people is due to the predominance of their prejudices. For the rest, even children do not lie without a reason, and on the whole they are more inclined to a love of truth than are their elders. If we were to reject little Hans's statements root and branch we should certainly be doing him a grave injustice. On the contrary, we can quite clearly distinguish from one another the occasions on which he was falsifying the facts or keeping them back under the compelling force of a resistance, the occasions on which, being undecided himself, he agreed with his father (so that what he said must not be taken as evidence), and the occasions on which, freed from every pressure, he burst into a flood of information about what was really going on inside him and about things which until then no one but he himself had known. Statements made by adults offer no greater certainty. It is a regrettable fact that no account of a psychoanalysis can reproduce the impressions received by the analyst as he conducts it, and that a final sense of conviction can never be obtained from reading about it but only from directly experiencing it. But this disability attaches in an equal degree to analyses made upon adults.

Little Hans is described by his parents as a cheerful, straightforward child, and so he should have been, considering the education given him by his parents, which consisted essentially in the omission of our usual educational sins. So long as he was able to carry on his researches in a state of happy *naïveté,* without a suspicion of the conflicts which were soon to arise out of them, he kept nothing back; and the observations made during the period before the phobia admit of no doubt or demur. It was with the outbreak of the illness and during the analysis that discrepancies began to make their appearance between what he said and what he thought; and this was partly because unconscious material, which he was unable to master all at once, was forcing itself upon him, and partly because the content of his thoughts provoked reservations on account of his relation to his parents. It is my unbiased opinion that these difficulties, too, turned out no greater than in many analyses made upon adults.

It is true that during the analysis Hans had to be told many things that he could not say himself, that he had to be presented with thoughts which he had so far shown no signs of possessing, and that his attention had to be turned in the direction from which his father was expecting something to come. This detracts from the evidential value of the analysis; but the procedure is the same in every case. For a psychoanalysis is not an impartial scientific investigation, but a therapeutic measure. Its essence is not to prove anything, but merely to alter something. In a psychoanalysis the physician always gives his patient (sometimes to a greater and sometimes to a less extent) the conscious anticipatory images by the help of which he is put in a position to recognize and to grasp the unconscious material. For there are some patients who need more of such assistance and some who need less; but there are none who get through without some of it. Slight disorders may perhaps be brought to an end by a person's unaided efforts, but never a neurosis—a thing which has set itself up against the ego as an element foreign to it. To get the better of such an element another person must be brought in, and in so far as that other person can be of assistance the neurosis will be curable. If it is in the very nature of any neurosis to turn away from the "other person"—and this seems to be one of the characteristics of the states grouped together under the name of dementia praecox— then for that very reason such a state will be incurable by any efforts of ours. Admittedly, then, a child, on account of the small development of its intellectual systems, requires especially energetic assistance. But, after all, the information which the physician gives his patient is itself derived in its turn from analytical experience; and indeed it is sufficiently convincing if, at the cost of this intervention by the physician, we are enabled to discover the structure of the pathogenic material and simultaneously to dissipate it.

And yet, even during the analysis, the small patient gave evidence of enough independence to acquit him upon the charge of "suggestion." Like all other children, he applied his childish sexual theories to the material before him without having received any encouragement to do so. These theories are extremely remote from the adult mind. Indeed, in this instance I actually omitted to warn Hans's father that the boy would be bound to approach the subject of childbirth by way of the excretory complex. This negligence on my part, though it led to an obscure phase in the analysis, was nevertheless the means of producing a good piece of evidence of the genuineness and independence of Hans's mental processes. He suddenly became occupied with "lumf," without his father, who is supposed to have been practising suggestion upon him, having the least idea how he had arrived at that subject or what was going to come of it. Nor can his father be saddled with any responsibility for the production of the two plumber phantasies, which arose out of Hans's early acquired "castration complex." And I must here confess that, out of theoretical interest, I entirely concealed from Hans's father my expectation that there would turn out to be some such connection, so as not to interfere with the value of a piece of evidence such as does not often come with one's grasp.

If I went more deeply into the details of the analysis I could produce plenty more evidence of Hans's independence of "suggestion;" but I shall break off the discussion of the first objection at this point. I am aware that even with this analysis I shall not succeed in convincing any one who will not let himself be convinced, and I shall proceed with my discussion of the case for the benefit of those readers who are already convinced of the objective reality of unconscious pathogenic material. And I do this with the agreeable assurance that the number of such readers is steadily increasing.

The first trait in little Hans which can be regarded as part of his sexual life was a quite peculiarly lively interest in his "widdler"—an organ deriving its name from that one of its two functions which, scarcely the less important of the two, is not to be eluded in the nursery. This interest aroused in him the spirit of inquiry, and he thus discovered that the presence or absence of a widdler made it possible to differentiate between animate and inanimate objects. He assumed that all animate objects were like himself, and possessed this important bodily organ; he observed that it was present in the larger animals, suspected that this was so too in both his parents, and was not deterred by the evidence of his own eyes from authenticating the fact in his new-born sister. One might almost say that it would have been too shattering a blow to his *"Weltanschauung"* if he had had to make up his mind to forgo the presence of this organ in a being similar to him; it would have been as though it were being torn away from himself. It was probably on this account that a threat of his mother's, which was concerned precisely with the loss of his widdler, was hastily dismissed from his thoughts and only succeeded in making its effects apparent at a later period. The reason for his mother's intervention had been that he used to like giving himself feelings of pleasure by touching his member: the little boy had begun to practise the commonest—and most normal—form of auto-erotic sexual activity.

The pleasure which a person takes in his own sexual organ may become associated with scoptophilia (or sexual pleasure in looking) in its active and passive forms, in a manner which has been very aptly described by Alfred Adler as "confluence of instincts."[1] So little Hans began to try to get a sight of other people's widdlers; his sexual curiosity developed, and at the same time he liked to exhibit his own widdler. One of his dreams, dating from the beginning of his repression period, expressed a wish that one of his little girl friends should assist him in widdling, that is, that she should share the spectacle. The dream shows, therefore, that up till then this wish had subsisted unrepressed, and later information confirmed the fact that he had been in the habit of gratifying it. The active side of his sexual scoptophilia soon became associated in him with a definite motive. He repeatedly expressed both to his father and his mother his regret that he had never yet seen their widdlers; and it was probably the need *for making a comparison* which impelled him to do this. The ego is always the standard by which one measures the outer world; one learns to understand it by means of a constant comparison with oneself. Hans had observed that large animals had widdlers that were correspondingly larger than his; he consequently suspected that the same was true of his parents, and was anxious to make sure of this. His mother, he thought, must certainly have a widdler "like a horse." He was then prepared with the comforting reflection that his widdler would grow with him. It was as though the child's wish to be bigger had been concentrated on his genitals.

[1] "Der Aggressionsbetrieb im Leben und in der Neurose" (1908).

Thus in little Hans's sexual constitution the genital zone was from the outset the one among his erotogenic zones which afforded him the most intense pleasure. The only other similar pleasure of which he gave evidence was excremental pleasure, the pleasure attached to the orifices through which urination and evacuation of the bowels are effected. In his final phantasy of bliss, with which his illness was overcome, he imagined he had children, whom he took to the W.C., whom he made to widdle, whose behinds he wiped, for whom, in short, he did "everything one can do with children"; it therefore seems impossible to avoid the assumption that during the period when he himself had been looked after as an infant these same performances had been the source of pleasurable sensations for him. He had obtained this pleasure from his erotogenic zones with the help of the person who had looked after him—his mother, in fact; and thus the pleasure already pointed the way to object-choice. But it is just possible that at a still earlier date he had been in the habit of giving himself this pleasure auto-erotically—that he had been one of those children who like retaining their excreta till they can derive a voluptuous sensation from their excavation. I say no more than that it is possible, because the matter was not cleared up in the analysis; the "making a row with the legs" (kicking about), of which he was so much frightened later on, points in that direction. But in any case these sources of pleasure had no particularly striking importance with Hans, as they so often have with other children. He early became clean in his habits, and neither bed-wetting nor diurnal incontinence played any part during his first years; no trace was observed in him of any inclination to play with his excrement, a propensity which is so revolting in adults, and which commonly makes its reappearance at the termination of processes of mental involution.

At this juncture it is as well to emphasize at once the fact that during his phobia there was an unmistakable repression of these two well-developed components of his sexual activity. He was ashamed of urinating before other people, accused himself of putting his finger to his widdler, made efforts to give up masturbating, and showed disgust at "lumf" and "widdle" and everything that reminded him of them. In his phantasy of looking after his children he did away again with this latter repression.

A sexual constitution like that of little Hans does not appear to carry with it a predisposition to the development either of perversions or of their negative (we will limit ourselves to a consideration of hysteria). As far as my experience goes, and there is still a real need for speaking with caution on this point) the innate constitution of hysterics —that this is also true of perverts is almost self-evident— is marked by the genital zone being relatively less prominent than the other erotogenic zones. But we must expressly except from this rule one particular "aberration" of sexual life. In those who later become homosexuals we meet with the same predominance in infancy of the genital zone (and especially of the penis) as in normal persons.[2] Indeed it is the high esteem felt by the homosexual for the male organ which decides his fate. In his childhood he chooses women as his sexual object, so long as he assumes that they too possess what in his eyes is an indispensable part of the body; when he becomes convinced that women have deceived him in this particular, they cease to be acceptable to him as a sexual object. He cannot forgo a penis in any one who is to attract him to sexual intercourse; and if circumstances are favourable he will fix his libido upon the "woman with a penis," a youth of feminine appearance. Homosexuals, then, are persons who, owing to the erotogenic importance of their own genitals, cannot do without a similar feature in their sexual object. In the course of their development from auto-erotism to object-love, they have remained at a point of fixation between the two.

There is absolutely no justification for distinguishing a special homosexual instinct. What constitutes a homo-

[2] As my expectations led me to suppose, and as Sadger's observations have shown, all homosexuals pass through an amphigenic phase in childhood.

sexual is a peculiarity not in his instinctual life but in his object-choice. Let me recall what I have said in my *Sexualtheorie* to the effect that we have mistakenly imagined the union between instinct and object in sexual life as being more intimate than it really is. A homosexual may have normal instincts, but he is unable to disengage them from a class of objects defined by a particular determinant. And in his childhood, since at that period it is taken for granted that this determinant is of universal application, he is able to behave like little Hans, who showed his affection to little boys and girls indiscriminately, and once described his friend Fritzl as "the girl he was fondest of." Hans was a homosexual (as all children may very well be), quite consistently with the fact, which must always be kept in mind, that he was *acquainted with only one kind of genital organ*—a genital organ like his own.[3]

In his subsequent development, however, it was not to homosexuality that our young libertine proceeded, but to an energetic masculinity with traits of polygamy; he knew how to vary his behaviour, too, with his varying feminine objects—audaciously aggressive in one case, languishing and bashful in another. His affection had moved from his mother on to other objects of love, but at a time when there was a scarcity in these it returned to her, only to break down in a neurosis. It was not until this happened that it became evident to what a pitch of intensity his love for his mother had developed and through what vicissitudes it had passed. The sexual aim which he pursued with his girl playmates, of sleeping with them, had originated in relation to his mother. It was expressed in words which might be retained in maturity, though they would

---

[3] (*Additional Note,* 1923.)—I have subsequently (1923) drawn attention to the fact that the period of sexual development which our little patient was passing through is universally characterized by acquaintance with only *one* sort of genital organ, namely, the male one. In contrast to the later period of maturity, this period is marked not by a genital primacy but by a primacy of the phallus.

then bear a richer connotation.[4] The boy had found his way to object-love in the usual manner from having been looked after when he was an infant; and a new pleasure had now become the most important for him—that of sleeping beside his mother. We should like to emphasize the importance of pleasure derived from cutaneous contact as a component in this new aim of Hans's, which, according to the nomenclature (artificial to our mind) of Moll, would have to be described as a satisfaction of the instinct of contrectation.

In his attitude towards his father and mother Hans confirms in the most concrete and uncompromising manner what I have said in my *Traumdeutung* and in my *Sexualtheorie* with regard to the sexual relations of a child to its parents. Hans was really a little Oedipus who wanted to have his father "out of the way," to get rid of him, so that he might be alone with his handsome mother and sleep with her. This wish had originated during his summer holidays, when the alternating presence and absence of his father had drawn Hans's attention to the condition upon which depended the intimacy with his mother which he longed for. At that time the form taken by the wish had been merely that his father should "go away"; and at a later stage it became possible for his fear of being bitten by a white horse to attach itself directly on to this form of the wish, owing to a chance impression which he received at the moment of some one else's departure. But subsequently (probably not until they had moved back to Vienna, where his father's absences were no longer to be reckoned on) the wish had taken the form that his father should be permanently away—that he should be "dead." The fear which sprang from this death-wish against his father, and which may thus be said to have had a normal motive, formed the chief obstacle to the analysis until it

---

[4] [The German *"bei jemandem schlafen,"* literally "to sleep with some one," is used (like the English "to lie with") in the sense of "to copulate."—*Trans.*]

was removed during the conversation in my consulting-room.[5]

But Hans was not by any means a young blackguard; he was not even one of those children in whom at his age the propensity towards cruelty and violence which is part of human nature still has free play. On the contrary, he had an unusually kind-hearted and affectionate disposition; his father reported that the transformation of aggressive tendencies into feelings of pity took place in him at a very early age. Long before the phobia he had become uneasy on seeing the horses in a merry-go-round being beaten; and he was never unmoved if any one wept in his presence. At one stage in the analysis a piece of suppressed sadism made its appearance in a certain context:[6] but it was *suppressed* sadism, and we shall presently have to discover from the context what it stood for and what it was meant to replace. And Hans deeply loved the father against whom he cherished these death-wishes; and while his intellect demurred to such a contradiction,[7] he could not help demonstrating the fact of its existence, by hitting his father and immediately afterwards kissing the place he had hit. We ourselves, too, must guard against making a difficulty of such a contradiction. The emotional life of man is in general made up of pairs of contraries such as these.[8]

---

[5] It is quite certain that Hans's two associations, "raspberry syrup" and "a gun for shooting people dead with," must have had more than one set of determinants. They probably had just as much to do with his hatred of his father as with his constipation complex. His father, who himself guessed the latter connection, also suggested that "raspberry syrup" might be related to "blood."

[6] His wanting to beat and tease horses.

[7] See the critical question he addressed to his father (p. 84).

[8] "Das macht, ich bin kein ausgeklügelt Buch.
   Ich bin ein Mensch mit seinem Widerspruch."
            C. F. MEYER, "Huttens letzte Tage."
   ["In fact, I am no clever work of fiction;
      I am a man, with all his contradiction."]

Indeed, if it were not so, repressions and neuroses would perhaps never come about. In the adult these pairs of contrary emotions do not as a rule become simultaneously conscious except at the climaxes of passionate love; at other times they usually go on suppressing each other until one of them succeeds in keeping the other altogether out of sight. But in children they can exist peaceably side by side for quite a considerable time.

The most important influence upon the course of Hans's psychosexual development was the birth of a baby sister when he was three and a half years old. That event accentuated his relations to his parents and gave him some insoluble problems to think about; and later, as he watched the way in which the infant was looked after, the memory-traces of his own earliest experiences of pleasure were revived in him. This influence, too, is a typical one: in an unexpectedly large number of life-histories, normal as well as pathological, we find ourselves obliged to take as our starting-point an outburst of sexual pleasure and sexual curiosity connected, like this one, with the birth of the next child. Hans's behaviour towards the new arrival was just what I have described in *Traumdeutung*.[9] In his fever a few days later he betrayed how little he liked the addition to the family. Affection for his sister might come later,[10] but his first attitude was hostility. From that time forward fear that yet another baby might arrive found a place among his conscious thoughts. In the neurosis, his hostility, already suppressed, was represented by a special fear—a fear of the bath. In the analysis he gave undisguised expression to his death-wish against his sister, and was not content with allusions which required supplementing by his father. His inner conscience did not consider this wish so wicked as the analogous one against his father; but it is clear that in his unconscious he treated both persons in the

[9] Seventh Edition, p. 174.

[10] Compare his plans of what he would do when his sister was old enough to speak (p. 112).

same way, because they both took his mummy away from him, and interfered with his being alone with her.

Moreover, this event and the feelings that were revived by it gave a new direction to his wishes. In his triumphant final phantasy he summed up all of his erotic wishes, both those derived from his auto-erotic phase and those connected with his object-love. In that phantasy he was married to his handsome mother and had innumerable children whom he could look after in his own way.

(II)

One day while Hans was in the street he was seized with an attack of morbid anxiety. He could not yet say what it was he was afraid of; but at the very beginning of this anxiety-state he betrayed to his father his motive for being ill, the advantage he derived from it (the paranosic gain). He wanted to stay with his mother and to coax with her; his recollection that he had also been separated from her at the time of the baby's birth may also, as his father suggests, have contributed to his longing. It soon became evident that his anxiety was no longer reconvertible into longing; he was afraid even when his mother went with him. In the meantime indications appeared of what it was to which his libido (now changed into anxiety) had become attached. He gave expression to an entirely specific fear that a white horse would bite him.

Disorders of this kind are called "phobias," and we might classify Hans's case as an agoraphobia if it were not for the fact that it is a characteristic of that complaint that the locomotion of which the patient is otherwise incapable can always be easily performed when he is accompanied by some specially selected person—in the last resort, by the physician. Hans's phobia did not fulfil this condition; it soon ceased having any relation to the question of locomotion and became more and more clearly concentrated upon horses. In the early days of his illness, when the anxiety was at its highest pitch, he expressed a fear that

"the horse'll come into the room," and it was this that
helped me so much towards understanding his condition.

In the classificatory system of the neuroses no definite
position has hitherto been assigned to "phobias." It seems
certain that they should only be regarded as syndromes
which may form part of various neuroses and that we need
not rank them as an independent disease entity. For
phobias of the kind to which little Hans's belongs, and
which are in fact the most common, the name of "anxiety-
hysteria" seems to me not inappropriate; I suggested the
term to Dr. W. Stekel when he was undertaking a description of neurotic anxiety-states,[11] and I hope it will come
into general use. It finds its justification in the similarity
between the psychological structure of these phobias and
that of hysteria—a similarity which is complete except
upon a single point. That point, however, is a decisive one
and well adapted for purposes of differentiation. For in
anxiety-hysteria the libido which has been liberated from
the pathogenic material by repression is not *converted*
(that is, diverted from the mental sphere into a somatic
innervation), but is set free in the shape of *anxiety*. In the
clinical cases that we meet with, this "anxiety-hysteria"
may be combined with "conversion-hysteria" in any
proportion. There exist cases of pure conversion-hysteria
without any trace of anxiety, just as there are cases of
simple anxiety-hysteria, which exhibit feelings of anxiety
and phobias, but have no admixture of conversion. The
case of little Hans is one of the latter sort.

Anxiety-hysterias are the most common of all psycho-
neurotic disorders. But, above all, they are those which
make their appearance earliest in life; they are *par excel-
lence* the neuroses of childhood. When a mother uses such
phrases as that her child's "nerves'" are in a bad state, we
can be certain that in nine cases out of ten the child is
suffering from some kind of morbid anxiety or from many
kinds at once. Unfortunately the finer mechanism of these
highly significant disorders has not yet been sufficiently

[11] *Nervöse Angstzustände und ihre Behandlung*, 1908.

studied. It has not yet been established whether anxiety-hysteria is determined, in contradistinction to conversion-hysteria and other neuroses, solely by constitutional factors or by accidental experiences, or by what combination of the two.[12] It seems to me that of all neurotic disorders it is the least dependent upon a special constitutional predisposition and that it is consequently the most easily acquired at any time of life.

One essential characteristic of anxiety-hysterias is very easily pointed out. An anxiety-hysteria tends to develop more and more into a "phobia." In the end the patient may have got rid of all his anxiety, but only at the price of subjecting himself to all kinds of inhibitions and restrictions. From the outset in anxiety-hysteria there is a constant effort of mind at work with the object of psychically binding the anxiety that has become liberated; but this work can neither effect a retransformation of the anxiety into libido, nor can it find a point of attachment in the same complexes which were the source of the libido. Nothing is left for it but to cut off access to every possible occasion that might lead to the development of anxiety, by erecting mental barriers in the nature of precautions, inhibitions, or prohibitions; and it is these defensive structures that appear to us in the form of phobias and that constitute to our eyes the essence of the disease.

The treatment of anxiety-hysteria may be said hitherto to have been a purely negative one. Experience has shown that it is impossible to effect the cure of a phobia (and even in certain circumstances dangerous to attempt to do so) by violent means, that is, by first depriving the patient of his defences and then putting him in a situation in which

---

[12] (*Additional Note*, 1923.)—The question which is raised here has not been pursued further. But there is no reason to suppose that anxiety-hysteria is an exception to the rule that both predisposition and experience must co-operate in the aetiology of a neurosis. Rank's view of the effects of the trauma of birth seems to throw special light upon the predisposition to anxiety-hysteria which is so strong in childhood.

he cannot escape the liberation of his anxiety. The result is that nothing can be done but to leave the patient to look for protection wherever he thinks he may find it; and he is merely regarded with a not very helpful contempt, on account of his "incomprehensible cowardice."

Little Hans's parents were determined from the very beginning of his illness that he was neither to be laughed at nor bullied, but that access must be obtained to his repressed wishes by means of psychoanalysis. The extraordinary pains taken by Hans's father were rewarded by success, and his reports will give us an opportunity of penetrating into the fabric of this type of phobia and of following the course of its analysis.

I think it is not unlikely that the extensive and detailed character of the analysis may have made it somewhat obscure to the reader. I shall therefore begin by giving a brief résumé of it, in which I shall omit all distracting side-issues and shall draw attention to the results as they came to light one after the other.

The first thing we learn is that the outbreak of the anxiety-state was by no means so sudden as appeared at first sight. A few days earlier the child had woken from an anxiety-dream to the effect that his mother had gone away, and that now he had no mother to coax with. This dream alone points to the presence of a repressive process of ominous intensity. We cannot explain it, as we can so many other anxiety-dreams, by supposing that the child had in his dream felt anxiety arising from some somatic cause and had made use of the anxiety for the purpose of fulfilling an unconscious wish which would otherwise have been deeply repressed.[13] We must regard it rather as a genuine punishment and repression dream, and, moreover, as a dream which failed in its function, since the child woke from his sleep in a state of anxiety. We can easily reconstruct what actually occurred in the unconscious. The child dreamed of exchanging endearments with his mother

---

[13] See my *Traumdeutung* (1900), Seventh Edition, p. 433.

and of sleeping with her; but all the pleasure was transformed into anxiety, and all the ideational content into its opposite. Repression had defeated the purpose of the dream-mechanism.

But the beginnings of this psychological situation go back further still. During the preceding summer Hans had had similar moods of mingled longing and apprehension, in which he had said similar things; and at that time they had secured him the advantage of being taken by his mother into her bed. We may assume that since then Hans had been in a state of intensified sexual excitement, the object of which was his mother. The intensity of this excitement was shown by his two attempts at seducing his mother (the second of which occurred just before the outbreak of his anxiety); and he found an incidental channel of discharge for it by masturbating every evening and in that way obtaining gratification. Whether the sudden exchange of this excitement into anxiety took place spontaneously, or as a result of his mother's rejection of his advances, or owing to the accidental revival of earlier impressions by the "exciting cause" of his illness (about which we shall hear presently)—this we cannot decide; and, indeed, it is a matter of indifference, for these three alternative possibilities cannot be regarded as mutually incompatible. The fact remains that his sexual excitement suddenly changed into anxiety.

We have already described the child's behaviour at the beginning of his anxiety, as well as the first content which he assigned to it, namely, that a *horse* would bite him. It was at this point that the first piece of therapy was interposed. His parents represented to him that his anxiety was the result of masturbation, and encouraged him to break himself of the habit. I took care that when they spoke to him great stress was laid upon his affection for his mother, for that was what he was trying to replace by his fear of horses. This first intervention brought a slight improvement, but the ground was soon lost again during a period of physical illness. Hans's condition remained unchanged. Soon afterwards he traced back his fear of being bitten by a horse to an impression he had received at Gmunden. A father had addressed his child on her departure with these words of warning: "Don't put your finger to the horse; if you do, it'll bite you." The words, "don't put your finger to," which Hans used in reporting this warning, resembled the form of words in which the warning against onanism had been framed. It seemed at first, therefore, as though Hans's parents were right in supposing that what he was frightened of was his own onanistic indulgence. But the whole nexus remained loose, and it seemed to be merely by chance that horses had become his bugbear.

I had expressed a suspicion that Hans's repressed wish might now be that he wanted at all costs to see his mother's widdler. As his behaviour to a new maid fitted in with this hypothesis, his father gave him his first piece of enlightenment, namely, that women have no widdlers. He reacted to this first effort at helping him by producing a phantasy that he had seen his mother showing her widdler.[14] This phantasy, and a remark made by him in conversation, to the effect that his widdler did grow on to him, allow us our first glimpse into the patient's unconscious mental processes. The fact was that the threat of castration made to him by his mother some fifteen months earlier was now having a deferred effect upon him. For his phantasy that his mother was doing the same as he had done (the familiar *tu quoque* repartee of inculpated children) was intended to serve as a piece of self-justification; it was a protective or defensive phantasy. At the same time we must remark that it was Hans's parents who had extracted from the pathogenic material operating in him the particular theme of his interest in widdlers. Hans followed their lead in this matter, but he had not yet taken any line of his own in the analysis. And no therapeutic success was to be observed. The analysis had passed far away from the subject of horses; and the information that women have no

[14] The context enables us to add: "and touching it" (p. 72). After all, he himself could not show his widdler without touching it.

widdlers was calculated, if anything, to increase his concern for the preservation of his own.

Therapeutic success, however, is not our primary aim; we endeavour rather to enable the patient to obtain a conscious grasp of his unconscious wishes. And this we can achieve by working upon the basis of the hints he throws out, and so, with the help of our interpretative technique, presenting the unconscious complex to his consciousness *in our own words*. There will be a certain degree of similarity between that which he hears from us and that which he is looking for, and which, in spite of all resistances, is trying to force its way through to consciousness; and it is this similarity that will enable him to discover the unconscious material. The physician is a step in front of him in knowledge; and the patient follows along his own road, until the two meet at the appointed goal. Beginners in psychoanalysis are apt to assimilate these two events, and to suppose that the moment at which one of the patient's unconscious complexes has become known to them is also the moment at which the patient himself recognizes it. They are expecting too much when they think that they will cure the patient by informing him of this piece of knowledge; for he can do no more with the information than make use of it to help himself in discovering the unconscious complex *where it is anchored* in his unconscious. A first success of this sort had now been achieved with Hans. Having partly mastered his castration complex, he was now able to communicate his wishes in regard to his mother. He did so, in what was still a distorted form, by means of the *phantasy of the two giraffes,* one of which was calling out in vain because Hans had taken possession of the other. He represented the "taking possession of" pictorially as "sitting down on." His father recognized the phantasy as a reproduction of a bedroom scene which used to take place in the morning between the boy and his parents; and he quickly stripped the underlying wish of the disguise which it still wore. The boy's father and mother were the two giraffes. The reason for the choice of a giraffe-phantasy for the purposes of disguise was fully explained by a visit that the boy had paid to those same large beasts at Schönbrunn a few days earlier, by the giraffe-drawing, belonging to an earlier period, which had been preserved by his father, and also, perhaps, by an unconscious comparison based upon the giraffe's long, stiff neck.[15] It may be remarked that the giraffe, as being a large animal and interesting on account of its widdler, was a possible competitor with the horse for the rôle of bugbear; moreover, the fact that both his father and his mother appeared as giraffes offered a hint which had not yet been followed up, as regards the interpretation of the anxiety-horses.

Immediately after the giraffe story Hans produced two minor phantasies: one of his forcing his way into a forbidden space at Schönbrunn, and the other of his smashing a railway-carriage window on the Stadtbahn. In each case the punishable nature of the action was emphasized, and in each his father appeared as an accomplice. Unluckily his father failed to interpret either of these phantasies, so that Hans himself gained nothing from telling them. In an analysis, however, a thing which has not been understood inevitably reappears; like an unlaid ghost, it cannot rest until the mystery has been solved and the spell broken.

There are no difficulties in the way of our understanding these two criminal phantasies. They belonged to Hans's complex of taking possession of his mother. Some kind of vague notion was struggling in the child's mind of something that he might do with his mother by means of which his taking possession of her would be consummated; for this elusive thought he found certain pictorial representations, which had in common the qualities of being violent and forbidden, and the content of which strikes us as fitting in most remarkably well with the hidden truth. We can only say that they were symbolic phantasies of coitus, and it was no irrelevant detail that his father was represented

[15] Hans's admiration of his mother's neck later on would fit in with this.

as sharing in his actions: "I should like," he seems to have been saying, "to be doing something with my mother, something forbidden; I do not know what it is, but I do know that you are doing it too."

The giraffe phantasy strengthened a conviction which had already begun to form in my mind when Hans expressed his fear that "the horse'll come into the room"; and I thought the right moment had now arrived for informing him that he was afraid of his father because he himself nourished jealous and hostile wishes against him —for it was essential to postulate this much with regard to his unconscious impulses. In telling him this, I had partly interpreted his fear of horses for him: the horse must be his father—whom he had good internal reasons for fearing. Certain details of which Hans had shown he was afraid, the black on horses' mouths and the things in front of their eyes (the moustaches and eyeglasses which are the privilege of a grown-up man), seemed to me to have been directly transposed from his father on to the horses.

By enlightening Hans on this subject I had cleared away his most powerful resistance against allowing his unconscious thoughts to be made conscious; for his father was himself acting as his physician. The worst of the attack was now over; there was a plentiful flow of material; the little patient summoned up courage to describe the details of his phobia, and soon began to take an active share in the conduct of the analysis.[16]

It was only then that we learnt what the objects and impressions were of which Hans was afraid. He was not only afraid of horses biting him—he was soon silent upon that point—but also of carts, of furniture-vans, and of buses (their common quality being, as presently became clear, that they were all heavily loaded), of horses that started moving, of horses that looked big and heavy, and of

[16] Even in analyses in which the physician and the patient are strangers, the fear of the father plays one of the most important parts as a resistance against the reproduction of the unconscious pathogenic material.

horses that drove quickly. The meaning of these specifica-
tions was explained by Hans himself: he was afraid of
horses *falling down,* and consequently incorporated in his
phobia everything that seemed likely to facilitate their
falling down.

It not at all infrequently happens that it is only after
doing a certain amount of psychoanalytic work with a
patient that an analyst can succeed in learning the actual
content of a phobia, the precise form of words of an obses-
sional impulse, and so on. Repression has not only de-
scended upon the unconscious complexes, but it is continu-
ally attacking their derivatives as well, and even prevents
the patient from becoming aware of the products of the
disease itself. The analyst thus finds himself in the position,
curious for a doctor, of coming to the help of a disease, and
of procuring it its due of attention. But only those who
entirely misunderstand the nature of psychoanalysis will
lay stress upon this phase of the work and suppose that
on its account harm is likely to be done by analysis. The
fact is that you must catch your thief before you can hang
him, and that it requires some expenditure of labour to
get securely hold of the pathological structures at the
destruction of which the treatment is aimed.

I have already remarked in the course of my running
commentary upon the case history that it is most instruc-
tive to plunge in this way into the details of a phobia, and
thus arrive at a conviction of the secondary nature of the
relation between the anxiety and its objects. It is this that
accounts for phobias being at once so curiously diffuse and
so strictly conditioned. Hans evidently collected the material for the particular disguises adopted by his fear from
the impressions to which he was all day long exposed
owing to the Head Customs House being situated on the
opposite side of the street. In this connection, too, he
showed signs of an impulse—though it was now inhibited
by his anxiety—to play with the loads on the carts, with
the packages, casks and boxes, like the street-boys.

It was at this stage of the analysis that he recalled the event, insignificant in itself, which immediately preceded the outbreak of the illness and may no doubt be regarded as the exciting cause of the outbreak. He went for a walk with his mother, and saw a bus-horse fall down and kick about with its feet. This made a great impression on him. He was terrified, and thought the horse was dead; and from that time on he thought that all horses would fall down. His father pointed out to him that when he saw the horse fall down he must have thought of him, his father, and have wished that he might fall down in the same way and be dead. Hans did not dispute this interpretation; and a little while later he played a game consisting of biting his father, and so showed that he accepted the theory of his having identified his father with the horse he was afraid of. From that time forward his behaviour to his father was unconstrained and fearless, and in fact a trifle overbearing. Nevertheless his fear of horses persisted; nor was it yet clear through what chain of associations the horse's falling down had stirred up his unconscious wishes.

Let us summarize the results that had so far been reached. Behind the fear to which Hans first gave expression, the fear of a horse biting him, we had discovered a more deeply seated fear, the fear of horses falling down; and both kinds of horses, the biting horse and the falling horse, had been shown to represent his father, who was going to punish him for the evil wishes he was nourishing against him. Meanwhile the analysis had moved away from the subject of his mother.

Quite unexpectedly, and certainly without any prompting from his father, Hans now began to be occupied with the "lumf" complex, and to show disgust at things that reminded him of evacuating his bowels. His father, who was reluctant to go with him along that line, pushed on with the analysis through thick and thin in the direction in which he wanted to go. He elicited from Hans the recollection of an event at Gmunden, the impression of which lay concealed behind that of the falling bus-horse. While they were playing at horses, Fritzl, the playmate of whom he was so fond, but at the same time, perhaps, his rival with his many girl friends, had hit his foot against a stone and had fallen down, and his foot had bled. Seeing the bus-horse fall had reminded him of this accident. It deserves to be noticed that Hans, who was at the moment concerned with other things, began by denying that Fritzl had fallen down (though this was the event which formed the connection between the two scenes) and only admitted it at a later stage of the analysis. It is especially interesting, however, to observe the way in which the transformation of Hans's libido into anxiety was projected on to the principal object of his phobia, on to horses. Horses interested him the most of all the large animals; playing at horses was his favourite game with the other children. I had a suspicion—and this was confirmed by Hans's father when I asked him—that the first person who had served Hans as a horse must have been his father; and it was this that had enabled him to regard Fritzl as a substitute for his father when the accident happened at Gmunden. When repression had set in and brought a revulsion of feeling along with it, horses, which had till then been associated with so much pleasure, were necessarily turned into objects of fear.

But, as we have already said, it was owing to the intervention of Hans's father that this last important discovery was made of the way in which the exciting cause of the illness had operated. Hans himself was occupied with his lumf interests, and thither at last we must follow him. We learn that formerly Hans had been in the habit of insisting upon accompanying his mother to the W.C., and that he had revived this custom with his friend Berta at a time when she was filling his mother's place, until the fact became known and he was forbidden to do so. Pleasure taken in looking on while some one one loves performs the natural functions is once more a "confluence of instincts," a phenomenon of which we have already noticed an instance in Hans. In the end his father went into the lumf symbolism, and recognized that there was an analogy between a heavily loaded cart and a body loaded with faeces, between the way in which a cart drives out through a gateway and the way in which faeces leave the body, and so on.

By this time, however, the position occupied by Hans in the analysis had become very different from what it had been at an earlier stage. Previously, his father had been able to tell him in advance what was coming, while Hans had merely followed his lead and come trotting after; but now it was Hans who was forging ahead, so rapidly and steadily that his father found it difficult to keep up with him. Without any warning, as it were, Hans produced a new phantasy: the plumber unscrewed the bath in which Hans was, and then stuck him in the stomach with his big borer. Henceforward the material brought up in the analysis far outstripped our powers of understanding it. It was not until later that it was possible to guess that this was a remoulding of a *phantasy of procreation,* distorted by anxiety. The big bath of water, in which Hans imagined himself, was his mother's womb; the "borer," which his father had from the first recognized as a penis, owed its mention to its connection with "being born." The interpretation that we are obliged to give to the phantasy will of course sound very curious: "With your big penis you 'bored' me" (*i.e.,* "gave birth to me") "and put me in my mother's womb." For the moment, however, the phantasy eluded interpretation, and merely served Hans as a point of connection from which to continue giving his information.

Hans showed fear of being given his bath in the big bath; and this fear was once more a composite one. One part of it escaped us as yet, but the other part could at once be elucidated in connection with his baby sister having her bath. Hans confessed to having wished that his mother might drop the child while it was being given its bath, so that it should die. His own anxiety while he was having his bath was a fear of retribution for this evil wish and of being punished by the same thing happening to him. Hans now left the subject of lumf and passed on directly to that of his baby sister. We may well imagine what this juxtaposition signified: nothing less, in fact, than that little Hanna was a lumf herself—that all babies were lumfs and were born like lumfs. We can now understand that all furniture-vans and drays and buses were only stork-box carts, and were only of interest to Hans as being symbolic representations of pregnancy; and that when a heavy or heavily loaded horse fell down he can have seen in it only one thing—a childbirth, a delivery [*"ein Nieder-kommen"*].[17] Thus the falling horse was not only his dying father but also his mother in childbirth.

And at this point Hans gave us a surprise, for which we were not in the very least prepared. He had noticed his mother's pregnancy, which had ended with the birth of his little sister when he was three and a half years old, and had, at any rate after the confinement, pieced the facts of the case together—without telling any one, it is true, and perhaps without being able to tell any one. All that could be seen at the time was that immediately after the delivery he had taken up an extremely sceptical attitude towards everything that might be supposed to point to the presence of the stork. *But that—in complete contradiction to his official speeches—he knew in his unconscious where the baby came from and where it had been before,* is proved beyond a shadow of doubt by the present analysis; indeed, this is perhaps its most unassailable feature.

The most cogent evidence of this is furnished by the phantasy (which he persisted in with so much obstinacy, and embellished with such a wealth of detail) of how Hanna had been with them at Gmunden the summer be-

[17] [See footnote, p. 134.]

fore her birth, of how she had travelled there with them, and of how she had been able to do far more then than she had a year later, after she had been born. The effrontery with which Hans related this phantasy and the countless extravagant lies with which he interwove it were anything but meaningless. All of this was intended as a revenge upon his father, against whom he harboured a grudge for having misled him with the stork fable. It was just as though he had meant to say: "If you really thought I was so stupid as all that, and expected me to believe that the stork brought Hanna, then in return I expect you to accept my inventions as the truth." This act of revenge on the part of our young inquirer upon his father was succeeded by the clearly correlated phantasy of teasing and beating horses. This phantasy, again, had two constituents. On the one hand, it was based upon the teasing to which he had submitted his father just before; and, on the other hand, it reproduced the obscure sadistic desires directed towards his mother, which had already found expression (though they had not at first been understood) in his phantasies of doing something forbidden. Hans even confessed consciously to a desire to beat his mother.

There are not many more mysteries ahead of us now. An obscure phantasy of missing a train seems to have been a forerunner of the later notion of handing over Hans's father to his grandmother at Lainz, for the phantasy dealt with a visit to Lainz, and his grandmother appeared in it. Another phantasy, in which a boy gave the guard 50,000 florins to let him ride on the truck, almost sounds like a plan of buying his mother from his father, part of whose power, of course, lay in his wealth. At about this time, too, he confessed, with a degree of openness which he had never before reached, that he wished to get rid of his father, and that the reason he wished it was that his father interfered with his own intimacy with his mother. We must not be surprised to find the same wishes constantly reappearing in the course of the analysis. The monotony only arises because the process of interpretation has been completed. For Hans they were not mere repetitions, but steps in a progressive development from timid hinting to fully conscious, undistorted perspicuity.

What remains are just such confirmations on Hans's part of analytical conclusions which our interpretations had already established. In an entirely unequivocal symptomatic act, which he disguised slightly from the maid but not at all from his father, he showed how he imagined a birth took place; but if we look into it more closely we can see that he showed something else, that he was hinting at something which was not alluded to again in the analysis. He pushed a small penknife which belonged to his mother in through a round hole in an india-rubber doll, and then let it drop out again by tearing apart the doll's legs. The enlightenment which he received from his parents soon afterwards, to the effect that children do in fact grow inside their mother's body and are pushed out of it like a lumf, came too late; it could tell him nothing new. Another symptomatic act, happening as though by accident, involved a confession that he had wished his father dead; for, just at the moment his father was talking of this death-wish, Hans let a horse that he was playing with fall down —knocked it over in fact. Further, he confirmed in so many words the hypothesis that heavily loaded carts represented his mother's pregnancy to him, and the horse's falling down was like having a baby. The most delightful piece of confirmation in this connection was his proving that, in his view, children were "lumfs" by inventing the name of "Lodi" for his favourite child. There was some delay in reporting this fact, for it then appeared that he had been playing with this sausage child of his for a long time past.[18]

We have already considered Hans's two concluding phantasies, with which his recovery was rounded off. One

[18] I remember a set of drawings by T. T. Heine in a number of *Simplicissimus,* in which that brilliant illustrator depicted the fate of the pork-butcher's child, who fell into the sausage

of them, that of the plumber giving him a new and, as his father guessed, a bigger widdler, was not merely a repetition of the earlier phantasy concerning the plumber and the bath. The new one was a triumphant wish-phantasy, and with it he overcame his fear of castration. His other phantasy, which confessed to the wish to be married to his mother and to have many children by her, did not merely exhaust the content of the unconscious complexes which had been stirred up by the sight of the falling horse and which had generated his anxiety. It also corrected that portion of those thoughts which was entirely unacceptable; for, instead of killing his father, it made him innocuous by promoting him to a marriage with Hans's grandmother. With this phantasy both the illness and the analysis came to an appropriate end.

While the analysis of a case is in progress it is impossible to obtain any clear impression of the structure and development of the neurosis. That is the business of a synthetic process which must be performed subsequently. In attempting to carry out such a synthesis of little Hans's phobia we shall take as our basis the account of his mental constitution, of his governing sexual wishes, and of his experiences up to the time of his sister's birth, which we have given in an earlier part of this paper.

The arrival of his sister brought into Hans's life many new elements, which from that time on gave him no rest. In the first place he was obliged to submit to a certain degree of privation: to begin with, a temporary separation from his mother, and later a permanent diminution in the amount of care and attention which he had received from her and which thenceforward he had to grow accustomed to sharing with his sister. In the second place, he experi-

---

machine, and then, in the shape of a small sausage, was mourned over by his parents, received the Church's blessing, and flew up to Heaven. The artist's idea seems a puzzling one at first, but the Lodi episode in this analysis enables us to trace it back to its infantile root.

enced a revival of the pleasures he had enjoyed when he was looked after as an infant; for they were called up by all that he saw his mother doing for the baby. As a result of these two influences his erotic needs became intensified, while at the same time they began to obtain insufficient satisfaction. He made up for the loss which his sister's arrival had entailed on him by imagining that he had children of his own; and so long as he was at Gmunden— on his second visit there—and could really play with these children he found a sufficient outlet for his affections. But after his return to Vienna he was once more alone, and set all his hopes upon his mother. He had meanwhile suffered another privation, having been exiled from his mother's bedroom at the age of four. His intensified erotic excitability now found expression in phantasies, by which in his loneliness he conjured up his playmates of the past summer, and in regular auto-erotic satisfaction obtained by a masturbatory stimulation of his genitals.

But in the third place his sister's birth stimulated him to an effort of thought which, on the one hand, it was impossible to bring to a conclusion, and which, on the other hand, involved him in emotional conflicts. He was faced with the great riddle of where babies come from, which is perhaps the first problem to engage a child's mental powers, and of which the riddle of the Theban Sphinx is probably no more than a distorted version. He rejected the proffered solution of the stork having brought Hanna. For he had noticed that months before the baby's birth his mother's body had grown big, that then she had gone to bed, and had groaned while the birth was taking place, and that when she got up she was thin again. He therefore inferred that Hanna had been inside his mother's body, and had then come out like a "lumf." He was able to imagine the act of giving birth as a pleasurable one by relating it to his own first feelings of pleasure in passing stool; and he was thus able to find a double motive for wishing to have children of his own: the pleasure of giving birth to them and the pleasure (the compensatory pleasure, as it were) of looking after them. There was nothing in all of this that could have led him into doubts or conflicts.

But there was something else, which could not fail to make him uneasy. His father must have had something to do with little Hanna's *birth,* for he had declared that Hanna and Hans himself were his children. Yet it was certainly not his father who had brought them into the world, but his mother. This father of his came between him and his mother. When he was there Hans could not sleep with his mother, and when his mother wanted to take Hans into bed with her, his father used to call out. Hans had learnt from experience how well off he could be in his father's absence, and it was only justifiable that he should wish to get rid of him. And then Hans's hostility had received a fresh reinforcement. His father had told him the lie about the stork and so made it impossible for him to ask for enlightenment upon these things. He not only prevented his being in bed with his mother, but also kept from him the knowledge he was thirsting for. He was putting Hans at a disadvantage in both directions, and was obviously doing so for his own benefit.

But this father, whom he could not help hating as a rival, was the same father whom he had always loved and was bound to go on loving, who had been his model, had been his first playmate, and had looked after him from his earliest infancy: and this it was that gave rise to the first conflict. Nor could this conflict find an immediate solution. For Hans's nature had so developed that for the moment his love could not but keep the upper hand and suppress his hate—though it could not kill it, for his hate was perpetually kept alive by his love for his mother.

But his father not only knew where children came from, he actually performed it—the thing that Hans could only obscurely divine. The widdler must have something to do with it, for his own grew excited whenever he thought of these things—and it must be a big widdler too, bigger than Hans's own. If he listened to these premonitory sensations he could only suppose that it was a question of some act

of violence performed upon his mother, of smashing something, of making an opening into something, or forcing a
way into an enclosed space—such were the impulses that
he felt stirring within him. But although the sensations in
his penis had put him on the road to postulating a vagina,
yet he could not solve the problem, for within his experience no such thing existed as his widdler required. On the
contrary, his conviction that his mother possessed a penis
just as he did stood in the way of any solution. His attempt at discovering what it was that had to be done with
his mother in order that she might have children sank down
into his unconscious; and his two active impulses—the
hostile one against his father and the sadistic-tender one
towards his mother—could be put to no use, the first because of the love that existed side by side with the hatred,
and the second because of the perplexity in which his infantile sexual theories left him.

This is how, basing my conclusions upon the results
of the analysis, I am obliged to reconstruct the unconscious
complexes and wishes, the repression and reawakening
of which produced little Hans's phobia. I am aware that
in so doing I am attributing a great deal to the mental
capacity of a child between four and five years of age; but
I have let myself be guided by what we have recently
learned, and I do not consider myself bound by the prejudices of our ignorance. It might perhaps have been possible to make use of Hans's fear of the "making a row
with the legs" for filling up a few more gaps in our adjudi-
cation upon the evidence. Hans, it is true, declared that it
reminded him of his kicking about with his legs when he
was compelled to leave off playing so as to do lumf; so
that this element of the neurosis becomes connected with
the problem whether his mother liked having children or
was compelled to have them. But I have an impression
that this is not the whole explanation of the "making a
row with the legs." Hans's father was unable to confirm
my suspicion that there was some recollection stirring in
the child's mind of having observed a scene of sexual inter-

course between his parents in their bedroom. So let us be content with what we have discovered.

It is hard to say what the influence was which, in the situation we have just sketched, led to the sudden change in Hans and to the transformation of his libidinal longing into anxiety—to say from which side it was that repression set in. The question could probably only be decided by making a comparison between this analysis and a number of similar ones. Whether the scales were turned by the child's *intellectual* inability to solve the difficult problem of the begetting of children and to cope with the aggressive impulses that were liberated by his approaching its solution, or whether the effect was produced by a *somatic* incapacity, a constitutional intolerance of the masturbatory gratification in which he regularly indulged (whether, that is, the mere persistence of sexual excitement at such a high pitch of intensity was bound to bring about a revulsion)— this question must be left open until fresh experience can come to our assistance.

Chronological considerations make it impossible for us to attach any great importance to the actual exciting cause of the outbreak of Hans's illness, for he had shown signs of apprehensiveness long before he saw the bus-horse fall down in the street.

Nevertheless, the neurosis attached itself directly on to this chance event and preserved a trace of it in the circumstance of the horse being exalted into the object of the anxiety. In itself the impression of the accident which he happened to witness carried no "traumatic force"; it acquired its great effectiveness only from the fact that horses had formerly been of importance to him as objects of his predilection and interest, from the fact that he associated the event in his mind with an earlier event at Gmunden which had more claim to be regarded as traumatic, namely, with Fritzl's falling down while he was playing at horses, and lastly from the fact that there was an easy path of association from Fritzl to his father. Indeed, even these connections would probably not have been sufficient if it had not been that, thanks to the pliability and ambiguity of associative chains, the same event showed itself capable of stirring the second of the complexes that lurked in Hans's unconscious, the complex of his pregnant mother's confinement. From that moment the way was clear for the return of the repressed; and it returned, in such a manner that *the pathogenic material was remodelled and transposed on to the horse-complex, while the accompanying effects were uniformly turned into anxiety.*

It deserves to be noticed that the ideational content of Hans's phobia as it then stood had to be submitted to one further process of distortion and substitution before his consciousness took cognizance of it. Hans's first formulation of his anxiety was: "the horse will bite me;" and this was derived from another episode at Gmunden, which was on the one hand related to his hostile wishes against his father and on the other hand was reminiscent of the warning he had been given against onanism. Some distracting influence, emanating from his parents perhaps, had made itself felt. I am not certain whether the reports upon Hans were at that time drawn up with sufficient care to enable us to decide whether he expressed his anxiety in this form *before* or not until *after* his mother had taken him to task on the subject of masturbating. I should be inclined to suspect that it was not until afterwards, though this would contradict the account given in the case history. At any rate, it is evident that at every point Hans's hostile complex against his father screened his lustful one about his mother, just as it was the first to be disclosed and dealt with in the analysis.

In other cases of this kind there would be a great deal more to be said upon the structure, the development, and the diffusion of the neurosis. But the history of little Hans's attack was very short; almost as soon as it had begun, its place was taken by the history of its treatment. And although during the treatment the phobia appeared to develop further and to extend over new objects and to lay down new conditions, his father, since he was himself treating the case, naturally had sufficient penetration to see that it was merely a question of the emergence of material that was already in existence, and not of fresh productions for which the treatment might be held responsible. In the treatment of other cases it would not always be possible to count upon so much penetration.

Before I can regard this synthesis as completed I must turn to yet another aspect of the case, which will take us into the very heart of the difficulties that lie in the way of our understanding of neurotic states. We have seen how our little patient was overtaken by a great wave of repression and that it caught precisely those of his sexual components that were dominant.[19] He gave up onanism, and turned away in disgust from everything that reminded him of excrement and of looking on at other people performing their natural functions. But these were not the components which were stirred up by the exciting cause of the illness (his seeing the horse falling down) or which provided the material for the symptoms, that is, the content of the phobia.

This allows us, therefore, to make a radical distinction. We shall probably come to understand the case more deeply if we turn to those other components which *do* fulfill the two conditions that have just been mentioned. These were tendencies in Hans which had already been suppressed and which, so far as we can tell, had never been able to find uninhibited expression: hostile and jealous feelings against his father, and sadistic impulses (premonitions, as it were, of copulation) towards his mother. These early suppressions may perhaps have gone to form the

[19] Hans's father even observed that simultaneously with this repression a certain amount of sublimation set in. From the time of the beginning of his anxiety Hans began to show an increased interest in music and to develop his inherited musical gift.

predisposition for his subsequent illness. These aggressive propensities of Hans's found no outlet, and as soon as there came a time of privation and of intensified sexual excitement, they tried to break their way out with reinforced strength. It was then that the battle which we call his "phobia" burst out. During the course of it a part of the repressed ideas, in a distorted form and transformed on to another complex, forced their way into consciousness as the content of the phobia. But it was a decidedly paltry success. Victory lay with the forces of repression; *and they made use of the opportunity to extend their dominion over components other than those that had rebelled.* This last circumstance, however, does not in the least alter the fact that the essence of Hans's illness was entirely dependent upon the nature of the instinctual components that had to be repulsed. The content of his phobia was such as to impose a very great measure of restriction upon his freedom of movement, and that was its purpose. It was therefore a powerful reaction against the obscure impulses to movement which were especially directed against his mother. For Hans horses had always typified pleasure in movement ("I'm a young horse," he had said as he jumped about); but since this pleasure in movement included the impulse to copulate, the neurosis imposed a restriction on it and exalted the horse into an emblem of terror. Thus it would seem as though all that the repressed instincts got from the neurosis was the honour of providing pretexts for the appearance of the anxiety in consciousness. But however clear may have been the victory in Hans's phobia of the forces that were opposed to sexuality, nevertheless, since such an illness is in its very nature a compromise, this cannot have been all that the repressed instincts obtained. After all, Hans's phobia of horses was an obstacle to his going into the street, and could serve as a means of allowing him to stay at home with his beloved mother. In this way, therefore, his affection for his mother triumphantly achieved its aim. In consequence of his phobia, the lover clung to the object of his love—though, to be sure, steps had been taken to make him innocuous. The true character of a neurotic disorder is exhibited in this twofold result.

Alfred Adler, in a suggestive paper,[20] has recently developed the view that anxiety arises from the suppression of what he calls the "aggressive instinct," and by a very sweeping synthetic process he ascribes to that instinct the chief part in human events, "in real life and in the neuroses." As we have come to the conclusion that in our present case of phobia the anxiety is to be explained as being due to the repression of Hans's aggressive propensities (the hostile ones against his father and the sadistic ones against his mother), we seem to have produced a most striking piece of confirmation of Adler's view. I am nevertheless unable to assent to it, and indeed I regard it as a misleading generalization. I cannot bring myself to assume the existence of a special aggressive instinct alongside of the familiar instincts of self-preservation and of sex, and on an equal footing with them.[21] It appears to me that Adler has mistakenly hypostatized into a special instinct what is in reality a universal and indispensable attribute of all instincts and impulses—their "impulsive" and dy-

[20] "Der Aggressionsbetrieb im Leben und in der Neurose" (1908). This is the same paper from which I have borrowed the term "confluence of instincts."

[21] (*Additional Note*, 1923.)—The above passage was written at a time when Adler seemed still to be taking his stand upon the ground of psychoanalysis, and before he had put forward the masculine protest and disavowed repression. Since then I have myself been obliged to assert the existence of an "aggressive instinct," but it is different from Adler's. I prefer to call it the "destructive" or "death instinct." See *Beyond the Pleasure Principle* (1920), and *Das Ich und das Es* (1923). Its opposition to the libidinal instincts finds an expression in the familiar polarity of love and hate. My disagreement with Adler's view, which results in a general characteristic of all instincts being encroached upon for the benefit of a single one of them, remains unaltered.

namic character, what might be described as their capacity for initiating motion. Nothing would then remain of the other instincts but their relation to an aim, for their relation to the means of reaching that aim would have been taken over from them by the "aggressive instinct." In spite of all the uncertainty and obscurity of our theory of instincts I should prefer for the present to adhere to the usual view, which leaves each instinct its own power of becoming aggressive; and I should be inclined to recognize the two instincts which became repressed in Hans as familiar components of the sexual libido.

(III)

I shall now proceed to what I hope will be a brief discussion of how far little Hans's phobia offers any contribution of general importance to our views upon the life and education of children. But before doing so I must return to the objection which has so long been held over, and according to which Hans was a neurotic, a "degenerate" with a bad heredity, and not a normal child, knowledge about whom could be applied to other children. I have for some time been thinking with pain of the way in which the adherents of "the normal person" will fall upon poor little Hans as soon as they are told that he can in fact be shown to have had a hereditary taint. His handsome mother fell ill with a neurosis as a result of a conflict during her girlhood. I was able to be of assistance to her at the time, and this had in fact been the beginning of my connection with Hans's parents. It is only with the greatest diffidence that I venture to bring forward one or two considerations in his favour.

In the first place Hans was not what one would understand, strictly speaking, by a degenerate child, condemned by his heredity to be a neurotic. On the contrary, he was well formed physically, and was a cheerful, amiable, active-minded young fellow who might give pleasure to more people than his own father. There can be no question, of course, as to his sexual precocity; but on that point there is very little material upon which a fair comparison can be based. I gather, for instance, from a piece of collective research conducted in America, that it is by no means such a rare thing to find object-choice and feelings of love in boys at a similarly early age; and the same may be learnt from studying the records of the childhood of men who have later come to be recognized as "great." I should therefore be inclined to believe that sexual precocity is a correlate of intellectual precocity, which is seldom absent, and that it is therefore to be met with in gifted children more often than might be expected.

Furthermore, let me say in Hans's favour (and I frankly admit my partisan attitude) that he is not the only child who has been overtaken by a phobia at some time or other in his childhood. Troubles of that kind are well known to be quite extraordinarily frequent, even in children the strictness of whose up-bringing has left nothing to be desired. In later life these children either become neurotic or remain healthy. Their phobias are shouted down in the nursery because they are inaccessible to treatment and are decidedly inconvenient. In the course of months or years they diminish, and the child seems to recover; but no one can tell what psychological changes are necessitated by such a recovery, or what alterations in character are involved in it. When, however, an adult neurotic patient comes to us for psychoanalytic treatment (and let us assume that his illness has only become manifest after he has reached maturity), we find regularly that his neurosis is connected on to an infantile anxiety such as we have been discussing, and is in fact a continuation of it; so that, as it were, a continuous and undisturbed thread of mental activity, taking its start from the conflicts of his childhood, has been spun through his life—irrespective of whether the first symptom of those conflicts has persisted or has retreated under the pressure of circumstances. I think, therefore, that Hans's illness may perhaps have been no more serious than that of many other children who are not branded as "degenerates;" but since he was brought up without being intimidated, and with as much consideration and as little coercion as possible, his anxiety dared to show itself more boldly. With him there was no place for such motives as a bad conscience or a fear of punishment, which with other children must no doubt contribute to making the anxiety less. It seems to me that we concentrate too much upon symptoms and concern ourselves too little with their causes. In bringing up children we aim only at being left in peace and having no difficulties, in short, at training up a model child, and we pay very little attention to whether such a course of development is for the child's good as well. I can therefore well imagine that it may have been to Hans's advantage to have produced this phobia; for it directed his parents' attention to the unavoidable difficulties by which a child is confronted when in the course of his cultural training he is called upon to overcome the innate instinctual components of his mind, and his trouble brought his father to his assistance. It may be that Hans now enjoys an advantage over other children, in that he no longer carries within him that seed in the shape of repressed complexes which must always be of some significance for a child's later life, and which undoubtedly brings with it a certain degree of deformity of character if not a predisposition to a subsequent neurosis. I am inclined to think that this is so, but I do not know if many others will share my opinion; nor do I know whether experience will prove me right.

But I must now inquire what harm was done to Hans by dragging to light in him complexes such as are not only repressed by children but dreaded by their parents. Did the little boy proceed to take some serious action as regards what he wanted from his mother? Or did his evil intentions against his father give place to evil deeds? Such misgivings will no doubt have occurred to many doctors, who misunderstand the nature of psychoanalysis and think that wicked instincts are strengthened by being made conscious. Wise men like these are being no more than consistent when they implore us for heaven's sake not to meddle with the evil things that lurk behind a neurosis. In so doing they forget, it is true, that they are physicians, and their words bear a fatal resemblance to Dogberry's, when he advised the watch to avoid all contact with any thieves they might happen to meet: "for such kind of men, the less you meddle or make with them, why, the more is for your honesty."[22]

On the contrary, the only results of the analysis were that Hans recovered, that he ceased to be afraid of horses, and that he got on to rather familiar terms with his father, as the latter reported with some amusement. But whatever his father may have lost in the boy's respect he won back in his confidence: "I thought," said Hans, "you knew everything, as you knew that about the horse." For analysis does not undo the *effects* of repression. The instincts which were formerly suppressed remain suppressed; but the same effect is produced in a different way. Analysis replaces the process of repression, which is an automatic and excessive one, by a temperate and purposeful control on the part of the highest mental faculties. In a word, *analysis replaces repression by condemnation.* This seems to bring us the long-looked-for evidence that consciousness has a biological function, and that with its entrance upon the scene an important advantage is secured.[23]

[22] At this point I cannot keep back an astonished question. Where do my opponents obtain their knowledge, which they produce with so much confidence, on the question whether the repressed sexual instincts play a part, and if so what part, in the aetiology of the neuroses, if they shut their patients' mouths as soon as they begin to talk about their complexes or their derivatives? For the only alternative source of knowledge remaining open to them are my own papers and those of my adherents.

[23] (*Additional Note,* 1923).—I am here using the word "consciousness" in a sense which I have since avoided, namely, to describe our normal processes of thought—such, that is, as are capable of entering consciousness. We know that thought

If matters had lain entirely in my hands, I should have ventured to give the child the one remaining piece of enlightenment which his parents withheld from him. I should have confirmed his instinctive premonitions, by telling him of the existence of the vagina and of copulation; thus I should have still further diminished his unsolved residue, and put an end to his stream of questions. I am convinced that this new piece of enlightenment would have made him lose neither his love for his mother nor his own childish nature, and that he would have understood that his preoccupation with these important, these momentous things must rest for the present—until his wish to be big had been fulfilled. But the pedagogic experiment was not carried so far.

That no sharp line can be drawn between "neurotic" and "normal" people—whether children or adults,—that our conception of "disease" is a purely practical one and a matter of degree, that predisposition and the eventualities of life must combine before the requisite degree can be reached, and that consequently a number of individuals are constantly passing from the class of healthy people into that of neurotic patients, while a far smaller number also make the journey in the opposite direction,—all of these are things which have been said so often and have met with so much agreement that I am certainly not alone in maintaining their truth. It is, to say the least of it, extremely probable that a child's education can exercise a powerful influence for good or for evil upon that predisposition which we have just mentioned as being one of the factors in the occurrence of "disease;" but what that education is to aim at and at what point it is to be

---

processes of this kind may also take place *preconsciously;* and it is wiser to regard their actual "consciousness" from a purely phenomenological standpoint. By this I do not, of course, mean to contradict the expectation that consciousness in this more limited sense of the word must also fulfil some biological function.

brought to bear seem at present to be very doubtful questions. Hitherto education has only set itself the task of controlling, or, it would often be more proper to say, of suppressing, the instincts. The results have been by no means gratifying, and where the process has succeeded it has only been to the advantage of a small number of favoured individuals who have not been required to suppress their instincts. Nor has any one inquired by what means and at what cost the suppression of the inconvenient instincts has been achieved. Supposing now that we substitute another task for this one, and aim instead at making the individual capable of becoming a civilized and useful member of society with the least possible sacrifice of his own activity; in that case the information gained by psychoanalysis, upon the origin of every nervous affection, can claim with justice that it deserves to be regarded by educators as an invaluable guide in their conduct towards children. What practical conclusions may follow from this, and how far experience may justify the application of those conclusions within our present social system, are matters which I leave to the examination and decision of others.

I cannot take leave of our small patient's phobia without giving expression to a notion which has made its analysis, leading as it did to a recovery, seem of especial value to me. Strictly speaking, I learnt nothing new from this analysis, nothing that I had not already been able to discover (though often less distinctly and more indirectly) from other patients analysed at a more advanced age. But the neuroses of these other patients could in every instance be traced back to the same infantile complexes that were revealed behind Hans's phobia. I am therefore tempted to claim for this neurosis of childhood the significance of being a type and a model, and to suppose that the multiplicity of the phenomena of repression exhibited by neuroses and the abundance of their pathogenic material do not prevent their being derived from a very limited number of processes concerned with identical ideational complexes.

4. Postscript (1922)[1]

A FEW MONTHS AGO—in the spring of 1922—a young man introduced himself to me and informed me that he was the "little Hans" whose infantile neurosis had been the subject of the paper which I published in 1909. I was very glad to see him again, for about two years after the end of his analysis I had lost sight of him and had heard nothing of him for more than ten years. The publication of this first analysis of a child had caused a great stir and even greater indignation, and a most evil future had been foretold for the poor little boy, because he had been "robbed of his innocence" at such a tender age and had been made the victim of a psychoanalysis.

But none of these apprehensions had come true. Little Hans was now a strapping youth of nineteen. He declared that he was perfectly well, and suffered from no troubles or inhibitions. Not only had he come through his puberty without any damage, but his emotional life had successfully undergone one of the severest of ordeals. His parents had been divorced and each of them had married again. In consequence of this he lived by himself; but he was on good terms with both of his parents; and only regretted that as a result of the breaking-up of the family he had been separated from the younger sister he was so fond of.

One piece of information given me by little Hans struck me as particularly remarkable; nor do I venture to give any explanation of it. When he read his case history, he told me, the whole of it came to him as something unknown; he did not recognize himself; he could remember nothing; and it was only when he came upon the journey to Gmunden that there dawned on him a kind of glimmering recollection that it might have been he himself that it happened to. So the analysis had not preserved the events from amnesia, but had been overtaken by amnesia itself. Any one who is familiar with psychoanalysis may oc-

[1] [First published in *Internationale Zeitschrift für Psychoanalyse*, Bd. viii., 1922.]

casionally experience something similar in sleep. He will be woken up by a dream, and will decide to analyse it then and there; he will then go to sleep again feeling quite satisfied with the result of his efforts; and next morning dream and analysis will alike be forgotten.

V

Infantile Mental Life

Two Lies Told by Children[1] (1913)

IT IS COMPREHENSIBLE that children should tell lies when
in doing so they mimic the lies of grown-up people. But
a number of the lies of well-brought-up children have a
peculiar significance, and should cause their instructors
to reflect rather than to be angry. These lies proceed from
the influence of an excessive love motive, and become
momentous if they lead to a misunderstanding between
the child and the person whom it loves.

1

A girl of seven (in her second year at school) had
asked her father for money to buy colours for painting
Easter eggs. The father had refused, saying he had no
money. Shortly afterwards the girl again asked for some
money for a contribution towards a wreath for the funeral
of the late reigning princess. Each of the school-children
was to bring fifty pfennigs. The father gave her ten marks;
she paid her contribution, put nine marks on her father's
writing-table, and with the remaining fifty pfennigs bought
paints, which she hid in her toy-cupboard.

At dinner the father asked suspiciously what she had
done with the missing pfennigs, and whether she had not
bought the colours with them. She denied it; but her
brother, who was two years older, and together with whom
she had planned to paint the eggs, betrayed her; the
colours were found in the cupboard. The father, very

[1] First published in *Zeitschrift*, Bd. I., 1913; reprinted in
Sammlung, Vierte Folge. [Translated by E. Colburn Mayne.]

angry, handed the culprit over to her mother for punishment, which was severely administered. Afterwards the mother herself was overwhelmed when she saw the child's extreme despair. She caressed the little girl after punishing her, and took her for a walk to console her. But the effects of this experience, described by the patient herself as the "turning-point" of her life, proved to be immitigable. She had hitherto been a wild, self-confident child; thenceforth she became timid and vacillating. During her engagement she flew into a rage that was incomprehensible even to herself, when her mother was buying furniture and trousseau-garments for her. She had the feeling that after all it was *her* money, and no one else ought to buy anything with it. As a young wife she was shy of asking her husband for any expenditure for her personal needs, and made an unnecessary distinction between "her" money and his. During the course of her treatment it happened now and again that her husband's remittances to her were delayed, so that she was resourceless in the foreign city. After she had once told me this, I made her promise that if it happened again she would borrow the small necessary sum from me. She gave the promise, but on the next occasion of embarrassment she did not keep it and preferred to pawn her jewellery. She explained that she could not take money from me.

The appropriation of the fifty pfennigs in her childhood had a significance which the father could not divine. Some time before she began going to school, she had played a singular little prank with money. A neighbour with whom she was friendly had sent the girl with a small sum of money, as companion for her own still younger little boy, to make some purchase in a shop. As the elder of the two, she was bringing the change from the purchase back to the house. But when she met the neighbour's servant-maid in the street, she flung the money down on the pavement. In the analysis of this action, even to herself inexplicable, the thought of Judas occurred to her, when he flung away the silver pieces gained by him through the betrayal of his Master. She declared that she was certainly acquainted with the story of the Passion before she went to school. But in what manner could she have identified herself with Judas?

At the age of three and a half she had a nursemaid of whom she was extremely fond. This girl had a love-affair with a doctor, and visited his surgery with the child. It appears that the child was the witness of various sexual proceedings. Whether she saw the doctor give money to the nursemaid is not certainly established; there is, however, no doubt that the girl gave the child little presents of money to ensure her silence, and that purchases (probably sweets) were made with these on the way home. It is possible, too, that the doctor himself occasionally gave money to the child. Nevertheless, the child betrayed the girl to her mother out of jealousy. She played so ostentatiously with the pfennigs she had brought home that the mother could not but ask: "Where did you get that money?" The maid was dismissed.

To take money from anyone had thus early come to mean for her the yielding of the body, the erotic relation. To take money from her father was equivalent to a declaration of love. The phantasy that her father was her lover was so seductive that the childish desire for colours for the Easter eggs was easily, by its aid, indulged in spite of the prohibition. But she could not confess to the appropriation of the money; she was obliged to disavow it, because the motive of the deed, unknown to herself, could not be confessed. The father's chastisement was thus a refusal of the tenderness offered him, a humiliation, and so it broke her spirit. During the treatment a period of severe depression ensued, the explanation of which led to her remembering the events described, when I was once obliged to copy that humiliation by asking her not to bring me any more flowers.

It will scarcely be necessary, for the psychoanalyst, to insist upon the fact that in this child's little experience we are confronted with one of those extremely common cases of persistence of early anal erotism in the later erotic life. Even the desire to paint the eggs with colours derives from the same source.

2

A woman, now very ill as the consequence of a disappointment in life, was in earlier years a particularly healthy, truth-loving, earnest and admirable girl, and became a tender-natured woman. But still earlier, in the first years of her life, she had been a wilful and discontented child, and though she developed fairly early into an excessively good and conscientious one, there were occurrences in her schooldays which, when she fell ill, caused her deep remorse and were regarded by her as proofs of fundamental depravity. Memory told her that she had frequently in those days bragged and lied. Once, on the way home, a schoolfellow boasted: "Yesterday we had ice at dinner." She answered: "Oh, we have ice every day." In reality she did not know what ice at dinner could mean; she knew ice only in the long blocks in which it is carted about, but she perceived that there was something grand in having it for dinner, and so she would not be excelled by her schoolfellow.

When she was ten years old they were given in their drawing-lesson the task of drawing a circle in free-hand. But she made use of the compasses, thus easily producing a perfect circle, and showed her achievement to her neighbour in class. The teacher came up, heard her boasting, discovered the marks of the compasses in the delineation of the circle, and took the girl to task. But she stubbornly denied it, would not be abashed by any proofs, and took refuge in sullen silence. The teacher conferred with her father; both were influenced by the girl's usual good behaviour to decide against any further notice of the occurrence.

This child's two lies were instigated by the same complex. As the eldest of five children, the little girl early manifested an unusually strong attachment to her father, which was destined in later years to wreck her happiness in life. But she could not long escape the discovery that her beloved father was not so great a personage as she was inclined to think him. He had to struggle against money-difficulties; he was not so powerful nor so distinguished as she had imagined. This departure from her ideal she could not put up with. Since, as women do, she based all her ambition upon the beloved man, it became a dominating idea with her that she must support her father against the world. So she boasted to her schoolfellows, in order not to have to belittle her father. When, later on, she learnt to translate ice for dinner by *"glace,"* the path lay open for her remorse about this reminiscence to take its course as a dread of pieces or splinters of glass.

The father was an excellent draughtsman, and had often enough called forth the delight and wonderment of the children by exhibitions of his skill. In her identification of herself with her father, she had in school drawn that circle which she could produce successfully only by underhand means. It was as though she wanted to boast: "Look here —see what my father can do!" The consciousness of guilt that hung round her excessive fondness for her father found its outlet in the attempted deception; a confession was impossible for the same reason that was given in the earlier observation—it could not but have been the confession of the hidden incestuous love.

We should not think lightly of such episodes in child-life. It would be a grave misconception to read into such childish errors the prognosis of a developing immortal character. Nevertheless, they are intimately connected with the powerful motivations of the childish soul, and are prophetic of tendencies which will take shape either in the later destiny or in a future neurosis.